CHRISTIANITY
AND THE CELTS

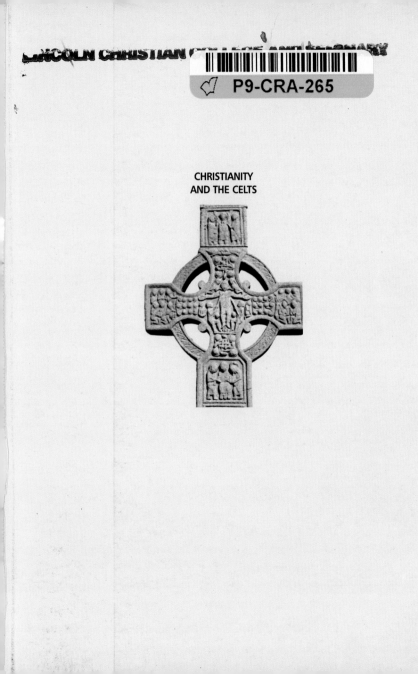

Christianity
and the Celts

Ted Olsen

Downers Grove, Illinois

The Ardagh Chalice, from the 7th or 8th century, is considered one of the finest examples of Celtic art.

Previous pages: Skellig Michael, an island 18 miles off Ireland's coast, remains one of the most isolated and preserved monastic sites.

Page one: Detail showing Christ's crucifixion from the 16-foot Muiredach Cross, which depicts scenes from the life of Christ. It still stands at the site of the Monasterboice monastery 1,100 years after its erection.

InterVarsity Press
P.O. Box 1400, Downers Grove, IL 60515-1426
World Wide Web: www.ivpress.com
E-mail: mail@ivpress.com

©2003 Ted Olsen

This edition copyright ©2003 Lion Publishing

Published in the United States of America by InterVarsity Press, Downers Grove, Illinois, with permission from Lion Publishing.

ISBN 0-8308-2357-3

Printed and bound in China

Library of Congress Cataloging-in-Publication Data has been requested

P 15 14 13 12 11 10 9 8 7 6 5 4 3 2 1

Y 11 10 09 08 07 06 05 04 03

Contents

'A Magic Bag' 6

1: 'The Whole Race is War Mad': Celtic Beginnings 10

2: Christianity in Early Britain 35

3: Patrick and the Conversion of Ireland 58

4: Ireland's Monks and Monasteries 79

5: Columba and Scotland 103

6: Out of, and Back into, the World 121

7: Resurrection and Raids 143

8: Celtic Christianity of the Non-Celts 167

Chronology 184

Suggestions for Further Reading 186

Index 188

Picture and Text Acknowledgments 191

728*

'A Magic Bag'

The Celts were warriors who sacked the great places of Europe – Rome in 390 BC, and Delphi almost a century later. They were also peace-loving saints, creating some of the first Western laws protecting non-combatants and granting rights to women.

The Celts were some of the most important scholars of history, not only copying countless tomes, but also writing their own works on history, geography, theology, and other subjects. However, Celts were also so secretive about their knowledge that they did not even allow a written language.

Celtic Christians were radically ascetic, submerging themselves in icy waters for hours and using themselves as oxen to pull their monastery's plough. Yet Celtic Christians also thought such radical asceticism was almost sinful – proof not of devotion to God, but of distance from him.

All of these statements were true to varying degrees at various times, and such paradoxes and contradictions make summarizing the Celts and their interaction with Christianity difficult. The problem is compounded by the flood of recent titles offering everything from *Celtic Spells and Wisdom for Self-Healing, Prosperity, and Great Sex* to *The Celtic Way of Evangelism*.

As J.R.R. Tolkien said, the term 'Celtic' is 'a magic bag, into which anything may be put, and out of which almost anything may come… Anything is possible in the fabulous Celtic twilight, which is not so much a twilight of the gods as of the reason.' He lamented this 'lunatic infection' long before Thomas Cahill's *How the Irish Saved Civilization*, *Riverdance* and Enya all became best-sellers.

That so much may be said of the Celtic world, however, does not mean that nothing should be said. Celtic wisdom may be trendy, but there remain important lessons for anyone willing to look. The best way to find them may not be in grand statements that cover all Celts from 700 BC to the modern era, but in stories of Celtic men and women from various eras.

Brennus, the Celtic commander who led the attack on Rome, would hardly have seen himself as kin to Columba, the royal monk who founded a monastery on the Scottish island of Iona in AD 562. The critical Gildas the Wise might have been upset at appearing in the same book as his contemporary David of Wales, whose self-mortification he found abhorrent. Yet all of these people were members of a kind of family, and without any of them the tale of Christianity and the Celts becomes too simple and ultimately incorrect.

An Irish monk, probably writing around the 9th century, understood the need to retell stories that he would rather avoid. Nevertheless, he copied for his contemporaries and future generations the pagan 'Táin Bó Cuailgne', an epic Celtic poem of bloody battles, mystical prophetesses, and cattle raiding. Still, he could not help adding his own postscript: 'I, who copied this history down, or rather this fantasy, do not believe in all the details. Several things in it are devilish lies. Others are the invention of poets. And others again have been thought up for the entertainment of idiots.'

Similarly, scholars have raised doubts about some of the stories retold here. It is not a new complaint; an Irish scholar in the 800s complained of 'the Irish habit of preferring fiction to true history'. But it is not this book's intention to rate the reliability of primary sources or catalogue the most current scholarly debates. (That is done well enough in any number of recent publications.)

This is less a book about 'Celtic Christianity' than it is about Christianity and Celts. Many similar books begin with the mission of Patrick to the Irish in the 5th century and end with Viking raids on monasteries in the 8th century. But Christianity touched Celtic lives on a much broader scale, from those living at the time of Jesus himself to today's speakers of Celtic languages in Ireland, Scotland, Wales, the Isle of Man, Brittany, and elsewhere.

Some of these believers were killed for their faith; others killed for it. Some confronted monsters, druids and demons; others fought their own weak flesh. Some travelled across the known world; others stayed cloistered in their monastery.

Around AD 793, Celtic monks began lamenting raids by strange tribes from the north. Nearly twelve centuries earlier, however, it was their Celtic forefathers who were seen as the northern raiders. This is where our stories begin.

The 8th-century Tara brooch represents the peak of Irish metallurgy.

CHAPTER 1

'The Whole Race is War Mad': Celtic Beginnings

'Their aspect is terrifying,' Greek historian Diodorus Siculus wrote of Celtic warriors in the 1st century BC:

They are very tall in stature, with rippling muscles under clear, white skin. Their hair is blonde, but not naturally so. They bleach it, to this day, artificially, washing it in lime and combing it back on their foreheads…
The Celtic way of fighting was alarming. They wore… bronze helmets with figures picked out on them, even horns, which make them look even taller than they already are… while others cover themselves with breast-armour made of chains. But most content themselves with the weapons nature gave them: they go naked into battle.

This 1st-century Celtic bronze helmet, found in the River Thames, was probably only for ceremonial use.

Alarming indeed. The army of Rome was literally scared to death when it first met a Celtic army from Gaul (an area of Western Europe mainly consisting of modern France and Belgium) at the Allia River on 18 July 390 BC. The Romans were so terrified, wrote the Roman historian Livy some time around the birth of Christ, that 'they fled, whole and unhurt, almost before they had seen their untried foe, without any attempt to fight or even to give back the battle-shout. None were slain while actually fighting; they were cut down from behind whilst hindering one another's flight in a confused, struggling mass.'

The Gauls were so stunned by this easy victory that they were almost certain it was a ruse; a sneak attack would follow at any moment. It did not. They continued the 12 miles southward to Rome, but upon finding the gates wide open, they were even surer of a trap. After a day's partying and resting, the Celtic Gauls continued cautiously into the city. Despite Celts' reputation for being violent barbarians, the actual invasion of Rome was a relatively calm, quiet affair. The residents had retreated to the fortified Capitol, leaving the city deserted. Now the Gauls were quite sure they were walking into a trap, and were 'appalled by the very desolation of the place'. Those who had scampered off to loot the empty houses quickly returned to seek the safety of numbers. Finally the Gauls came across some residents. Nine old patricians who had been refused the safety of the Capitol (they were certain to perish anyway, their fellow Romans reasoned) had put on their fanciest clothing and sat motionless, awaiting their fate. In fact, so strange was this encounter that the Gauls wondered if the gentry were really human.

'This race of men from the plains were all the harder, for hard land had borne them; built on stronger and firmer bones, and endowed with mighty sinew, they were a race undaunted by heat or cold, plague, or strange new foodstuffs.'

LUCRETIUS,
*ON THE NATURE
OF THINGS*

A brief stroke of one of the statues' long beards gave the answer. The insulted old Roman, Marcus Papirius, responded by rapping the offending Gaul with his ivory staff. The Gauls were immediately inflamed again with the passions of war, slew the old men, and soon prepared to invade the Capitol.

The Capitol, however, was not as easy a victory as the battlefield of Allia. An initial attack, unwisely made by hastily charging up the Forum's steep hill, was a costly error. A second, sneak attack in the dead of night was unluckily foiled by a skittish flock of sacred geese in the temple of Juno; and a blockade began to go very badly. Seven months after they had entered the city, the Celts found that their greatest enemy was not the sword, but malaria and other diseases. 'They died off like sheep,' Livy recorded. So many died from the pestilence that the Gauls gave up burying their dead. Finally, the Celtic commander, Brennus, convinced the Romans to offer a hefty ransom for their lives: half a ton of gold. But even after the Romans raised the sum, tensions flared between the nations. The Gauls, the Romans complained, were using biased weights. Brennus could not believe his ears. Angry at the hubris but eager to leave, he threw his sword upon the scales. '*Vae Victis!*' he shouted. 'Woe to the vanquished!'

Brennus and his soldiers left the city, concluding the first and only Celtic invasion of Rome. But battles, conquests, and dealings between the Celts and the eternal city would continue for centuries – even long after popes replaced emperors as Rome's most powerful citizens.

Through outsiders' eyes

George Orwell's famous line, 'History is written by the winners,' does not hold true in this case. The Celts left no written record of their siege of Rome or of almost anything else in their long story. Thus it is mainly through Greek and Roman eyes that we first glimpse these far-ranging tribes, called *keltoi* (strangers, or hidden) by the former

A Gallic warrior from the time of the Gallic War (front) and his British counterpart. Watercolour by Peter Connolly.

and *galli* by the latter. They are heavily biased reports, of course, but nearly unified in how they perceived their northern neighbours.

'The whole race is war mad, high spirited, and quick to battle, but otherwise straightforward and not of evil character,' wrote the Greek historian Strabo, a contemporary of Diodorus. Both authors relied heavily on Stoic philosopher Poseidonius, who wrote a century earlier, for their information on the Celts:

At any time or place and on whatever pretext you stir them up, you will have them ready to face danger, even if they

Celtic art, such as this jug handle from the 5th or 4th century BC, often used the human head as its inspiration.

Table manners

Even when blood was not spilled, dinner could be an unsightly mess in the eyes of any Greek or Roman visitor. Diodorus detailed how beards were worn short, but moustaches were grown so long that they covered the Celtic men's mouths. 'Consequently,' he lamented, 'when they are eating, their moustaches become entangled in the food, and when they are drinking, the beverage passes, as it were, through a kind of strainer.' Poseidonius also fussed that though the Celts ate cleanly, they were 'like lions, raising up whole limbs in both hands and biting off the meat'. And always meat – large amounts of animal flesh, boiled in a cauldron or roasted on a spit, served with small portions of bread and gallons upon gallons of alcohol. 'The Gauls are exceedingly addicted to the use of wine,' Diodorus said, 'drinking it unmixed, and since they partake of this drink without moderation by reason of their craving for it, when they become drunk they fall into a stupor or into a maniacal rage.' A wheat-and-honey beer was poured freely among the lower classes. Indeed, the tribes became renowned for liquor – one of the only times Plato ever referred to Celts was to name them among six peoples overly fond of drinking – and Italian wine merchants were happy to take advantage of the situation, sometimes commanding a slave for each libation.

'They also invite strangers to their banquets, and only after the meal do they ask who they are and of what they stand in need.'

DIODORUS SICULUS, *HISTORICAL LIBRARY*

*have nothing on their side but their own strength and
courage. On the other hand, if won over by gentle persuasion
they willingly devote their energies to useful pursuits and
even take to a literary education… To the frankness and
high-spiritedness of their character must be added the traits
of childish boastfulness and love of decoration. They wear
ornaments of gold, torques on their necks, and bracelets on
their arms and wrists, while people of high rank wear dyed
garments sprinkled with gold. It is this vanity which makes
them unbearable in victory and so completely downcast in
defeat.*

It was not just the warring men who were like this.
'Nearly all the Gauls are of a lofty stature, fair and ruddy
complexion: terrible from the sternness of their eyes,
very quarrelsome, and of great pride and insolence,' said
Ammianus Marcellinus, the last major Roman historian
(c. AD 330–95):

*A whole troop of foreigners would not be able to withstand a
single Celt if he called his wife to his assistance. The wife is
even more formidable. She is usually very strong, and with
blue eyes; in rage her neck veins swell, she gnashes her teeth,
and brandishes her snow-white robust arms. She begins to
strike blows mingled with kicks, as if they were so many
missiles sent from the string of a catapult.*

The Celts were no less animated off the battlefield, if there
was such a place as off the battlefield. 'It is their custom,'
wrote Diodorus, 'even during the course of the meal, to
seize upon any trivial matter as an occasion for keen
disputation and then to challenge one another to single
combat, without any regard for their lives.' Diodorus's
source, Poseidonius (whose works are no longer available),
was also quoted by Athenaeus:

*They gather in arms and engage in mock battles, and fight
hand-to-hand, but sometimes wounds are inflicted, and the*

'Slashed with
axe or sword,
they kept their
desperation
while they
breathed;
pierced by
arrow or javelin,
they did not
abate of their
passion so long
as life remained.
Some drew
out from their
wounds the
spears, by which
they had been
hit, and threw
them at the
Greeks or used
them in close
fighting.'

PAUSANIAS,
*DESCRIPTION
OF GREECE*

A Pictish woman,
as imagined by
John White (active
c. 1570–93).

irritation caused by this may even lead to killing unless the bystanders restrain them. And in former times, when the hindquarters were served up the bravest hero took the thigh piece, and if another man claimed it they stood up and fought in single combat to death.

The Celts were not just brutish, barbarian enemies to the classical world; they were also potential allies. Just a few years after Brennus and his men left Rome, the tyrannical Dionysius of Syracuse hired Celts to aid the Spartans during the Peloponnesian War. A few decades later, in 335 BC, an increasingly cocky Alexander the Great met with some Celtic chieftains who lived near the Adriatic Sea. Fishing for flattery, the Macedonian king asked what they were most afraid of, expecting that they would answer 'You, my lord', or at least give some indication that his fame had spread to their country. 'We fear nothing but that they sky might fall on our heads,' they answered. Despite his disappointment ('They are vainglorious,' he dismissively complained later), Alexander struck a deal with them. The Celtic chiefs would side with Alexander – unless the sky fell on their heads. The oath was apparently a common Celtic vow; centuries later it was still being used in Christian Ireland.

Other Celtic tribes were still on the offensive, sacking the Greek holy places of Delphi in 279 BC, but the tides quickly turned. Slavic tribes began driving Celts out of Eastern Europe, and the Roman military eventually grew far stronger than the frightened bumblers Brennus had met at Allia. The famous military consul Gaius Marius began conquering Celtic territories around 101 BC. His nephew, Julius Caesar, soon followed. The general was interested in more than just the Celts' land, however. Whether for his own legacy or out of a genuine interest in knowledge (likely more of the former than the latter), Caesar attempted to serve as anthropologist as well as conqueror. As he began to claim Gaul for himself, driving the Celts either into subjugation or retreat, he wrote of

'We have no word for the man who is excessively fearless; perhaps one may call such a man mad or bereft of feeling, who fears nothing, neither earthquakes nor waves, as they say of the Celts.'

ARISTOTLE,
NICOMACHEAN
ETHICS

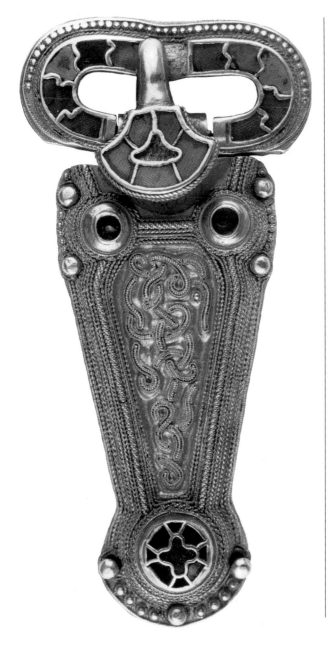

This Anglo-Saxon
belt buckle,
from about 620,
demonstrates
that Celtic art
and ideas still
held sway even
when Celts had
been conquered.

their lifestyle, their politics and their religion. But neither he nor the other classical writers gave much thought to where the Gauls and other Celts came from, besides the obvious answer 'over the Alps'. A Greek belief held that the Celts were descendants of Hercules. Celtus, the first of the *keltoi*, was the offspring of the strongman and Celtina, daughter of Britannus.

Genesis beyond the Alps

Today, historians and archaeologists are unsure about when and where the Celts emerged as a distinct culture. Many, in fact, argue that any thought of the Celts as a people group should be utterly rejected. Instead, they say, *Celtic* only applies to the family of languages various tribes spoke. Indeed, Celts were unified more by their language than by most cultural categories; they had no common king, no common country, no common creed. Furthermore, that they were unified by tongue is not insignificant or incidental. The Celts placed a high value on their language, so much so, in fact, that they feared the written word. It was not that they did not know their stories could be written down – enough contact with the classical world would have made clear at least some of the value of literacy – it was that they did not *want* them written down. (An illiterate culture was not totally uncommon at the time; historian Peter Ellis argues that Irish became only the third of Europe's written languages.) Much has been made of the history of Celtic languages and how they developed from their Indo-European parent, which also sired the Germanic, Romance, Slavonic and other language families. Linguists also enjoy pointing to how the Celtic tongue forked at some point, splitting the Brythonic (Welsh, Cornish), or P-Celtic, from the Goidelic (Irish, Scottish) Q-Celtic. The Welsh word for 'son', *mab*, is very similar to the Irish *mac*, for example, but 'children' (*plentyn* and *clann*, respectively) and other words are even more divergent.

The language-only historians and linguists have a

'They lived in unwalled villages, without any superfluous furniture, for... they slept on beds of leaves and fed on meat and were excessively occupied with war and agriculture.'

POLYBIUS,
THE HISTORIES

point, which serves as a counterbalance to the non-scholarly Celtic enthusiasts who would like to believe in a single – and usually utopian – culture wiped out by inconsiderate oppressors. Most Celts, especially those on the continent, likely saw themselves as members of their particular tribal nation rather than as part of 'the Celts'. But they shared more than linguistic similarities, starting from their apparent birth in the Alpine urnfield. Some time after 1000 BC, the people of the Harz mountains in what is now Germany shared a similar culture – the most archaeologically significant aspect of which is their cremation of the dead (hence the urnfield). This culture, also given to much jewellery, bright costumes, partying and fighting, apparently gave birth to a Celtic culture. Within 300 years, the Iron Age had come to the Celts, and they took advantage of it with zeal. They were Europe's first smiths, inventing impressive agricultural tools and weapons – including the important iron-wheeled chariot. But the Celts were not satisfied simply with the *usefulness* of iron ploughshares, reapers, and spears. In 1857, a wealthy would-be archaeologist in La Tène, Switzerland, began unearthing hundreds of weapons, tools, and other objects from the mud beneath Lake Neuchâtel. What they revealed gave evidence to Strabo's remark on the Celts' 'love of decoration' (and evidence against Polybius's comment that 'they had no knowledge whatsoever of any art or science'). From horse harnesses to sword hilts, nearly everything was lavishly decorated with swirls, flowers, and abstract designs. Soon the discovery of several other archaeological sites would demonstrate that such ornamentation was common, but historians still refer to this period of Celtic (if not completely pan-Celtic) culture, which lasted from about 450 BC to 15 BC, as La Tène.

During this time, the Celts spread throughout Europe and their influence spread even further. Modern maps attempting to illustrate the expansive Celtic areas give the impression of a massive hegemony – an apparent Celtic empire reaching from southern Spain to Turkey, from the

'The Gauls, imprisoned as they were by the Alps… first found a motive for overflowing into Italy from the circumstance of a Gallic citizen [who] brought with him when he came back some dried figs and grapes and some samples of oil and wine: consequently we may excuse them for having sought to obtain these things even by means of war.'

PLINY,
NATURAL HISTORY

Celtic culture had
its roots at Lake
Hallstatt and
La Tène, but by
200 BC, the Celtic
language was
spoken across
much of Europe.

The Hallstatt graves

Only 11 years before the discovery at La Tène, archaeologists began uncovering an even earlier trove of early Celtic artefacts by Austria's Lake Hallstatt. Over the next 16 years, 980 bodies were discovered, several in elaborate and well-stocked graves. The earliest of these remains dated from around 1200 BC, when the local economy was based on mining rock-salt. But the salt proved even more valuable to the modern archaeologists than it did these prehistoric residents: it preserved clothing, equipment,

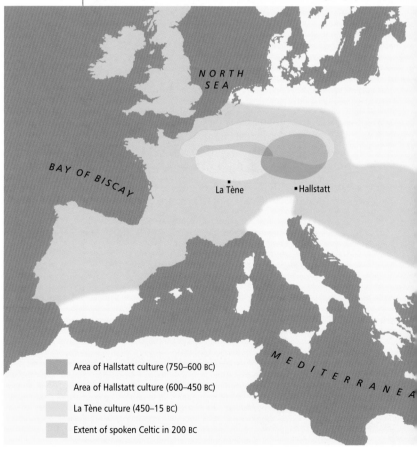

NORTH SEA

BAY OF BISCAY

■ La Tène   ■ Hallstatt

MEDITERRANEA

Area of Hallstatt culture (750–600 BC)

Area of Hallstatt culture (600–450 BC)

La Tène culture (450–15 BC)

Extent of spoken Celtic in 200 BC

and even a miner or two. Not all the discoveries at Hallstatt were Celtic, however, especially the earliest ones. But it is likely that most of the Iron Age remains from about 700 BC – including pottery, jewellery, wagons and massive, two-handed, double-edged swords with decorated hilts – were from dominantly Celtic tribes.

**Grave
excavations at
Hallstatt during
the mid-19th
century were
meticulously
recorded in
watercolour by
Johann Georg
Ramsauer.**

Atlantic Ocean to the Black Sea. Add in archaeological digs where Celtic artefacts have been found – an area stretching from Denmark to India – and they seem like some of the most successful conquerors the world has ever seen. But Celtic expansion cannot be seen through the same prism as organized military conquests such as Attila the Hun or Julius Caesar. It was gradual, the result of immigration at least as much as invasion, and most importantly, it was unorganized. As Caesar himself noted, the Celts were 'too much given to faction' to have organized a world conquest. Caesar and other expansionists exploited this propensity for dissension, first using tribal warfare to their advantage, then simply paying tribes to assist in battle against their fellow Celtic neighbours. Before they knew it, Europe belonged to the Romans they had once nearly vanquished.

Julius Caesar, conqueror and chronicler of the Celts of Gaul.

The fall of Celtic Europe

Caesar was by no means the only (or even the greatest) reason the Celts lost dominance in their lands. Fate had turned against them centuries before. But he was certainly responsible for the conquest of Gaul, the land most associated with the continental Celts. Ironically, it began almost by chance: the senatorial nobleman was assigned governorship over Gallia Transalpina (the Celtic area between Roman Italy and the Alps) after the sudden death of another. But Caesar was nothing if not opportunistic. He seized upon a request to drive back the Celtic Helvetti tribe – whose westward migration would potentially destabilize the region – and never looked back. By his own accounts, his conquering of the Helvetti cost more than 250,000 lives. But he was not done yet. Illegally, he continued through Gaul, slaughtering and displacing Celtic tribes that would not subjugate themselves to the man who would become *pontifex maximus*. Gaul was not enough; in 55 BC Caesar led his soldiers across the Channel into Britain. Ostensibly, Caesar was attempting to mete punishment for aid to the Gauls, but he likely had more conquest in mind. In any case, control of Gaul would be easier to maintain if he did not have to worry about British Celts. But, as historian

Vercingetorix's revolt

After Caesar's unsuccessful invasion of Britain, Celts throughout Gaul rose against him in 52 BC. Their leader was Vercingetorix, a young and headstrong nobleman of Arvernia (now central France). 'A man of boundless energy, he terrorized waverers with the rigours of an iron discipline,' Caesar wrote of him. Indeed, even after the Celtic warlord lost his first few battles, the tribal armies did not falter. When Caesar unsuccessfully attacked the Arvernian stronghold of Gergovia, however, it looked like the tide had turned. The Gauls had real hope of defeating the Romans. Even the neighbouring Aedui tribe, long-time Roman allies, defected and cut Caesar off from his supplies. But the Romans quickly rebounded, and Vercingetorix retreated to the hilltop defences at Alesia. It was the wrong move. Caesar surrounded the hill with elaborate siege works, with an inner set trapping Vercingetorix's forces and an outer set defending the Roman army against reinforcements (which came nearly a quarter of a million soldiers strong, but could not budge Caesar's 50,000 men). Caesar records that Vercingetorix summoned a council and told his fellows, 'I did not undertake the war for private ends, but in the cause of national liberty. And since I must now accept my fate, I place myself at your disposal. Make amends to the Romans by killing me or surrender me alive as you think best.' They chose surrender. The Romans imprisoned Vercingetorix for six years, then marched him through the capital to his ritual execution. Vercingetorix's rebellion was not the last revolt the Gauls would make against Caesar, but it was their last real challenge of him.

'They are wont to change their abode on slight provocation, migrating in bands with all their battle-array, or rather setting out with their households when displaced by a stronger enemy.'

STRABO, *GEOGRAPHY*

Norman Davies summarizes, 'He came; he saw; he did not conquer: but he took hostages, withdrew, and claimed a triumph. He headed south for the Alps, and fatefully recrossed the frontier of the Roman Republic on the Rubicon – his point of no return.' The historian Plutarch wrote that one million men died during Caesar's conquest of Gaul. A million more had been enslaved.

Early Celtic religion

All this time, Caesar continued to write his *Gallic War*, a propaganda piece intended to justify his conquests of Gaul despite his lack of orders to do so. But advertisement as it was, the work (also known as *Commentaries*) contains fascinating detail about Gallic life, especially Celtic religion. He wrote:

The whole nation of the Gauls is greatly devoted to ritual observances, and for that reason those who are smitten with the more grievous maladies and who are engaged in the perils of battle either sacrifice human victims or vow to do so, employing the druids as ministers for such sacrifices. They believe, in effect, that unless a man's life be paid, the majesty of the immortal gods may not be appeased.

The conqueror detailed such sacrifices in gory detail. One description, which later gained even wider circulation when Victorian-era artists began representing it graphically, explained how dozens of people would be locked into a giant wooden effigy, then burned alive. But this was likely imaginative or speculative. What is more certain – though there are still many historians who contest it – is that some kinds of human sacrifice took place among the Celts. And clearer still is the strong death motif in Celtic religious life. Roman proto-anthropologists and historians may have cribbed each other's notes on such matters, but almost all who wrote about the Celts were fascinated by the stories of human sacrifice. As Strabo wrote:

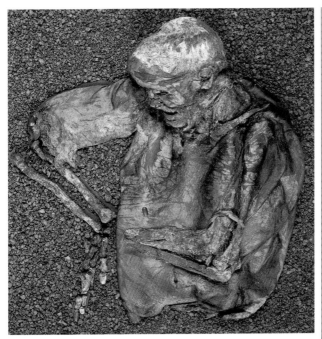

The 1st-century
Lindow Man,
sometimes called
Lovernius ('Fox-
man'), is so well
preserved that
upon its discovery
in 1984, police
initially thought
it was a modern-
day murder
victim.

They used to strike a human being, whom they had devoted to death, in the back with a sword, and then divine from his death-struggle. We are told of still other kinds of human sacrifices; for example, they would shoot victims to death with arrows, or impale them in the temples...

Of course, the classical world had its own gruesome traditions, and it may be that what was perceived as religious sacrifice may have been nothing more than ritualized capital punishment. The famous Lindow Man, pulled from the peat of Lindow Moss, ten miles from Manchester, England, has been cited as proof of sacrifice since his discovery in 1984. When he died, about 2,000 years ago, his killers were eager to make sure he was dead. They hit him on the head three times with an axe, tied a cord around his neck (twisting it with a stick until it acted as a garrotte), broke his neck, then slit his throat and tossed him into a bog. That Lindow Man apparently subjected himself to such treatment without a struggle and ate mistletoe (associated with the druids) before the killing does suggest that he was a kind of willing participant. But historians and archaeologists still disagree about whether he was a religious sacrifice.

Classical writers also confused the basics of pagan Celtic religion. Caesar wrote that their beliefs were 'much like those of other nations', and even assumed that the effigies he saw represented Mercury and other Roman gods. Other early historians assumed that the 'pantheon' of Celtic gods was organized like their own system. But the Celtic religious beliefs were hardly organized at all. A god regarded as extremely important to one Celtic tribe may not have been recognized at all by another, or may have been worshipped under a different name. History has left us with the names of 375 Celtic gods; all but 70 only appear once in extant writings. And even of these little is known. Dagda, the Irish 'Good God' ('good' meaning 'powerful' rather than 'beneficent') carries a club and cauldron, and was apparently venerated – at least in some parts – as the giant father or ruler of the other gods. Cernunnos, 'the horned one', was a Gaulish god of animals. Lugh 'of the long arm', whose importance is reflected in town names such as Lyons, Leiden, and Léon, ruled over arts and skills. The horse goddess Epona, who even became popular in the Roman cavalry in Gaul, may have been associated with fertility, but that seems to be said of almost every female deity.

These gods had the ability to change shape at will, usually adopting the shape of animals. When appearing in more human form, they often appeared in male and female pairs, but more importantly presented themselves in triples. One god often had two counterparts, might have three names, or might even be depicted with three heads.

But the gods were only one part of Celtic supernatural beliefs. They also venerated sacred animals (especially boars, dogs and birds), sacred places (springs, oddly shaped rocks, old trees), and sacred dates (one of which,

'The Gauls likewise make use of diviners, accounting them worthy of high approbation, and these men foretell the future by means of the flight or cries of birds and of the slaughter of sacred animals, and they have all the multitude subservient to them.'

DIODORUS SICULUS,
HISTORICAL LIBRARY

the festival of Samhain, still appears on modern calendars as Halloween).

The Celts also found supernatural significance in the human head, which classical writers found abhorrent. 'They cut off the heads of enemies slain in battle and attach them to the necks of their horses,' wrote Diodorus:

The blood-stained spoils they hand over to their attendants and carry off as booty, while striking up a paean and singing a song of victory; and they nail up these first fruits upon their houses just as do those who lay low wild animals in certain kinds of hunting. They embalm in cedar-oil the heads of their most distinguished enemies and preserve them carefully in a chest, and display them with pride to strangers, saying that for this head one of their ancestors,

The Gundestrup caldron, thought to be from the 2nd or 1st century BC, depicts several Celtic deities and animals.

or his father, or the man himself, refused the offer of a large sum of money. They say that some of them boast that they refused the weight of the head in gold.

But these were not headhunters merely seeking trophies. The Celts believed that the essence of a person was in their head – even after death. Thus skulls were even used to adorn temples.

Although druids are often depicted in white robes, as in this 1815 painting, they almost certainly did not wear them. *An Arch Druid in His Judicial Habit* by Robert Havell.

Propagating and unifying all these beliefs were the most famous of the pre-Christian Celts, the druids. Caesar was particularly interested in this brotherhood, noting that its members

… are concerned with divine worship, the due performance of sacrifices, public and private, and the interpretation of ritual questions: a great number of young men gather about them for the sake of instruction and hold them in great honour. In fact, it is they who decide in almost all disputes, public and private; and if any crime has been committed, or murder done, or there is any dispute about succession or boundaries, they also decide it, determining awards and penalties.

The druids, then, were not the mere priests so often portrayed in white hooded robes. They were also judges, teachers, healers, politicians and astronomers. Strabo called them 'the most just of men', noting that they were often the ones to broker peace between warring parties. But these men, exempt from military service as well as taxation, could also be responsible for starting battles – elections for chief druid sometimes ended in bloodshed.

'They profess to know the size and shape of the world, the movements of the heavens and the stars, and the will of the gods,' wrote Pomponius Mela, a Spaniard of the 1st century AD. But we will not know the details of these beliefs, because, as Caesar noted, 'The druids think it unlawful to commit this knowledge of theirs to writing.' They certainly knew how to write – Caesar notes their ability to write in Greek – but he attributes their prohibition to a desire for secrecy and a belief that writing weakens the memory.

On this point, Caesar conceded. 'Indeed it does generally happen that those who rely on written documents are less industrious in learning by heart and have a weaker memory,' he wrote. But he could afford to be so generous: he was, after all, driving their society from the continent.

Of course, Celts were not entirely wiped off the face of continental Europe by Caesar and his armies. Although many of the Celts simply chose to become Romanized, pockets of Celtic society still existed, such as Galatia. Rome had long approved of Celtic control in this area (now Turkey) – it helped to destabilize the region, keeping Eastern threats from encroaching on Roman territory. In the early 1st century BC, Rome and Galatia were even allies against Mithridates VI of Pontus. By 25 BC, Galatia was a Roman province, but it maintained much of its Celtic character. Four centuries later, Jerome (considered the most learned of the Latin church fathers) noted in his commentary on Paul's epistle to the Galatians that the area was still very Celtic. 'While the Galatians, in common with the whole East, speak Greek, their own language is almost identical with that of the Treviri [a Celtic tribe of eastern Gaul],' he wrote. And Caesar's observation that the Celts were 'too much given to faction' was still true in Jerome's day: 'Any one who has seen by how many schisms Ancyra [Ankara], the metropolis of Galatia, is rent and torn, and by how many differences and false doctrines the place is debauched, knows this as well as I do… The traces of the ancient foolishness remain to this day.'

'Not only the Druids, but others as well, say that men's souls, and also the universe, are indestructible, although both fire and water will at some time or other prevail over them.'

STRABO,
GEOGRAPHY

The first Celtic Christians

Was Paul's letter to the Galatians directed at one of the
first Celtic churches? There is some disagreement among
New Testament and Celtic scholars, but most believe that
Paul's epistle was written to the Romanized churches in
the south (where Paul visited), not the Celtic north. Others,
however, note that the apostle addresses his readers as
'Galatians', 'suggesting that they were a people, not just
inhabitants of a province'. This was certainly the view of
early commentators, including Jerome. Furthermore, the
province was under Roman rule but the capital, which Paul
may have been addressing, was still a Celtic stronghold.

Perhaps it is best for the legacy of Celtic Christianity
that its entry into recorded history does not begin with
Paul's chastising, 'You foolish Galatians! Who has bewitched
you?' If the epistle was not addressed to a Celtic church, it is
of little matter. Celtic Christians appear in reliable records
within a century of the apostle's death.

Medieval Christians believed that converting the Celts
had been a high priority for the early church: so much so
that the major figures of the Gospels had personally taken
Christianity into Gaul and beyond. According to legends,
no less than Mary, Lazarus, and Mary Magdalene were
the first missionaries to Gaul, founding the church in
Provence, by the Mediterranean Sea. *The Life of St Martial*
tells the story of one of Jesus' original 72 disciples who
was present at the resurrection of Lazarus and served the
food at the last supper. After baptizing this Martial, Peter
reportedly sent him to convert the Gauls. It is nonsense,
of course: this account was written in the 11th century to
make the 3rd-century – not 1st-century – Martial more
popular. (And it worked: Martial's relics in Limoges,
France, became among the most venerated in Europe.)

Christianity probably first came to Celts the way
it first came to most of the rest of the world: through
informal contacts by 'everyday' Christians, most likely
traders, whose names are lost. A few names of early
Christian Celts, however, do survive.

The first of these comes from the church in Lyons, which enters reliable history in martyrdom. As we have already seen, the city had been founded in honour of the Celtic god Lugh (the original name of the city was Lugdunum, 'Lugh's fort'), but Romans had long since captured the city and made it the capital of Gaul. In AD 12, Lyons became the centre for the worship of Emperor Augustus. As the Christians would later supplant pagan holidays such as Samhain and Saturnalia with observances of All Saints Day and Christmas, so the Romans replaced the 1 August Celtic celebrations of Lugnasadh with the Roman feast of the divine emperor.

How the church in Lyons was founded remains unknown, but when persecution began under Marcus Aurelius in AD 177, it was apparently the only organized church in Gaul (though it had already planted a second congregation in Vienne). Its ethnic make-up is also unclear, but at least one young member was a Celtic Gaul – Vettius Epagathus. According to a letter from the survivors of the pogrom that left 48 Christians dead, Vettius was 'a man filled with love for God and his neighbour... zealous for God and fervent in spirit'. He also, despite his youth, had some clout in the community and attempted to defend his fellow Christians when they came under attack. At first, Christians were excluded from the baths, markets and other public places. But mobs soon began pursuing the believers even in their homes. Soon Christians were rounded up, arrested and brought before the governor. It was here that Vettius attempted to come to their defence – but he ended up imprisoned with them. The aged bishop, Pothinus (thought to be originally from Asia Minor), was beaten and died of his wounds two days later. Blandina, the young servant of another martyr, is also considered by reputable historians to have been Celtic. She was, according to the letter, 'filled with such power, that those who tortured her one after the other in every way from morning till evening were wearied and tired... Her declaration, "I am a Christian, and there is no evil done amongst us," brought her refreshment, rest, and insensibility to all the sufferings inflicted on her.' Others were tortured to death, roasted in an iron seat, or (like Blandina) fed to wild beasts in the amphitheatre. The bodies of the 48 martyrs were exposed for six days, then burned, and the ashes thrown into the Rhône.

Celtic Christians such as Blandina, along with fellow believers of other nations, met their end here, in the Roman amphitheatre at Lyons.

The tragic persecution of the Christians and the death of the 92-year-old Pothinus led to the elevation of Irenaeus, one of the most important Christian writers of the 2nd century and the earliest recorded missionary to the Celts. Having escaped the massacre due to an errand to Rome, Irenaeus (from Asia Minor, like his predecessor) returned to Lyons to write one of the most influential apologetic works of the early church: *Against Heresies*. His five-volume treatise not only refuted such teachings as Gnosticism (the belief that the body and the whole physical world are evil), but also set forth much of the basis of Christian theology. While the Gnostics argued that they had a 'secret knowledge', Irenaeus argued that true belief was found in the teaching of the apostles, continued and guarded by elders and bishops. This argument, in which he listed the succession of Roman bishops as an example, would eventually set the basis for the hierarchy of the church. Irenaeus was also influential in determining the biblical canon, and was first to promote the four Gospels.

But Irenaeus was more than just a theologian – he was also a missionary. Though the bulk of his flock spoke Latin and Greek, the bishop made regular treks into the countryside to preach among the still-Celtic tribes. Indeed, he uses this as an excuse to the readers of *Against Heresies*:

You will not expect from me, a resident among the Celts, and mostly accustomed to a barbarous language, rhetorical skill, which I have never learned, nor power in writing, which I have not acquired, nor beauties of language and style, which I am not acquainted with.

A year or so after the martyrdoms at Lyons, Marcus Aurelius's persecution of Christians was felt by another Celt, Symphorian of Autun. A 5th-century account of his beheading tells how he was encouraged by his Christian mother in her native Gaulish language.

As Christianity continued to spread throughout the Roman world, it also continued to spread through Gaul. Frankish bishop and historian Gregory of Tours (539–94) says that Rome in AD 250 sent seven bishops to establish churches in Gaul. These were likely important additions to an already expanding church. Around this time, Cyprian of Carthage had already been drawn into controversy in the area over whether lapsed Christians could be readmitted to the church, and was pushing for the excommunication of the bishop of Arles.

But with each passing day, the churches in Gaul were less Celtic. Members of the churches may have had tribal blood, and some use of the Celtic languages continued until about AD 500. But it was clear that in almost all areas of culture, Rome had conquered the 'barbarians'. This was especially true in the cities, where Christianity first took root: though far less so in the countryside, where vestiges of Celtic and Greco-Roman paganism continued. Illustrating this difference, a local rhetorician in 395 told a story about a pagan peasant surprised at the power of the cross, 'the sign of that God who alone is worshiped in the large cities'.

In time, however, Rome would also lose control of Gaul, and even the name would disappear, taking instead the name of the Frankish foreigners from the other side of the Rhine. Roman Christianity would continue in the cities, but converting the countryside was a job that went largely unfulfilled. That is, until the Celts returned as Christian missionaries like Columbanus.

Christianity in Early Britain

It may seem unbelievable that Mary, Lazarus, and Mary Magdalene personally took the gospel of the resurrected Christ to the Celts of Gaul. Or that a mysterious disciple seemed to appear at every key recorded moment in the Gospels and then set about founding churches through what is now France. But consider the legend England prided itself on for centuries – that the church there was founded by Jesus himself. As ridiculous as it sounds, such a tale was invoked in British disputes with French churches over ascendancy and in Protestant arguments that Rome had nothing to do with the English church. It is unclear how much Christian mystic, artist, and poet William Blake (1757–1827) believed the tale, but his question remains famous (and later became that popular nationalistic hymn, 'Jerusalem'):

And did those feet in ancient time
  walk upon England's mountains green?
And was the holy Lamb of God
  on England's pleasant pastures seen?

According to widespread legends, Joseph of Arimathea, the 'good and just' Jewish leader who petitioned Pilate for Jesus' crucified body, was also Jesus' great-uncle (Mary's uncle). When Mary, Joseph and 12-year-old Jesus went to Jerusalem for Passover, Joseph supposedly housed them – and afterwards took the boy on a tin-trading trip to Glastonbury. Other legends say Jesus returned to the town as an adult to build a home and worked as a ship's

'The churches of France and Spain must yield in points of antiquity and precedence to that of Britain, as the latter church was founded by Joseph of Arimathea immediately after the passion of Christ.'

COUNCIL OF BASLE, 1434

carpenter. Older legends – though still unreliable – leave Jesus near the Mediterranean and send Joseph to Britain alone three decades after Jesus' ascension to heaven. Around the year 1240, someone added an introduction to *The Antiquity of the Church of Glastonbury*, written by English historian and monk William of Malmesbury a century before. It tells of how the apostle Philip sent Joseph and 11 others to Britain, where they encountered resistance from 'the barbaric king and his people', but were allowed to establish a church at Glastonbury 'because they came from afar'.

A century after the addition to William's history, John of Glastonbury expanded the Joseph legends, making him into an ancestor of King Arthur and the bearer of 'two cruets, white and silver, filled with the blood and sweat of the prophet Jesus'. This last detail was expanded even further by later legend-makers to make Joseph's prized cargo the Holy Grail itself.

Reliable early historians do not credit Joseph – or anyone else in particular – for bringing Christianity to Britain. They knew only that Christianity somehow made it there. 'In all parts of Spain, among the diverse nations of the Gauls, in regions of the Britons beyond Roman sway but subjected to Christ... the name of Christ now reigns,' North African apologist Tertullian wrote in *An Answer to the Jews* some time around AD 200. His contemporary Origen wrote that Christianity had not just come to the northern lands, it had become entirely accepted there. 'When before the coming of Christ,' he asked rhetorically, 'did the land of Britain agree on the worship of one God?' Renowned church historian Eusebius takes note of 'some apostles' who 'passed over the ocean to what are called the British Isles.' Most surprising is a remark by the 6th-century British monk Gildas (whom we shall meet shortly). 'These islands received their beams of light – that is, the holy precepts of Christ – the true Sun, as we know, at the latter part of the reign of Tiberius Caesar,' he claims in *The Ruin and*

'The divine goodness of our Lord and Saviour is equally diffused among the Britons, the Africans, and other nations of the world.'

ORIGEN OF
ALEXANDRIA

Conquest of Britain (*De Excidio Britanniae*). Modern scholars dismiss the comment – Tiberius was smothered to death in his bed in AD 37.

Tiberius was followed by Caligula, then Claudius. In AD 43, two years after Claudius was hailed as emperor of Rome, about 40,000 Roman soldiers finally achieved Julius Caesar's once-thwarted plan to invade Britain. Times had changed; Claudius invaded the island mainly because he could, and he needed the prestige of military victory. Having landed on the coast of Kent, the armies gradually subdued Wales and England, but found themselves overextended after a few victories against the Picts of Scotland.

Hadrian's Wall

By the middle of the 2nd century AD, about one of every eight Roman soldiers was stationed in Britain. But with even 50,000 troops on the island, the Romans could not conquer it all. In the 120s, Emperor Hadrian ordered the building of his great wall, stretching 76 miles down the valleys of the Tyne and Solway rivers. It was more symbolic than defensive, however; any serious attack by the Picts would have found it only a nuisance. Nor was the wall the northernmost extent of the Roman empire: other outposts lay beyond, and a generation later Antoninus Pius built a wall even further north. Hadrian's wall did, however, control the flow of movement and information between cultures, much like the Berlin Wall did in the 20th century.

The British Celts adapted quickly to the lifestyle of their Roman conquerors. Celtic languages were abandoned in favour of Latin, and Celts began bowing to the gods of the Roman pantheon. The antlered Cernunnos still had his devotees, and other Celtic gods were simply Romanized (Apollo Belenos, for example), but the emperor cult became a new addition to Celtic worship.

Britain's first martyr

It was because of this new Romanized British religion that we first learn the name of a British Christian: Alban. It is

even impossible to know exactly when he lived – perhaps centuries after Christianity first came to the island. We do know that he was not the first Christian in Britain – his own story precludes it.

Alban enters history a pagan, but a hospitable one. He welcomed into his home a Christian priest who was fleeing persecution. Exactly which persecution is a matter of debate. Anglo-Saxon church historian Bede says it was that of Diocletian (284–305), but the Caesar of Gaul and Britain at that time, Constantius Chlorus, is famous for his toleration of Christians. More likely, the story occurred during the reign of Decius (c. 249–51) or even Septimus Severus (c. 193–211). It would have mattered little to the priest which emperor was responsible for his death warrant.

Previous pages: Snow covers Hadrian's Wall, an 80-mile effort 'to separate the Romans from the Barbarians' in Britain.

He simply knew that he needed a hiding place.

It did not take long for the priest's religious devotion to influence Alban. Soon, writes Bede, 'Alban renounced the darkness of idolatry and sincerely accepted Christ.' According to another legend, no sooner had Alban knelt in prayer than soldiers appeared at the door, having been informed of the priest's location. Though the legends differ on timing, all agree that the new convert swapped clothes with his spiritual father, donning the priest's hooded cloak. It was not until Alban was brought before the judge (who was then reportedly attending a pagan sacrifice) that his identity was revealed. 'Since you have chosen to conceal a sacrilegious rebel rather than deliver him to the soldiers for his well-deserved punishment for blasphemy,' the judge said angrily, 'you shall undergo all the punishment due to him.' The judge gave one way out – make a sacrifice to the idols. Alban refused. 'What is your family and race?' asked the judge. 'What does that concern you?' Alban responded. 'If you want to know the truth about my religion, know that I am a Christian, and practise Christian rites.' 'I demand to know your name!' 'My parents named me Alban. And I worship and adore the living and true God, who created all things.'

Again the judge ordered Alban to sacrifice to the pagan gods, but again Alban refused, saying whoever did so is

An early 13th-century illustration of Alban's martyrdom, in which the executioner's eyes can be seen falling from their sockets.

'doomed to the pains of hell'. When beatings and whippings could not change his mind, he was sentenced to death by decapitation.

The tales of the journey to the execution hill and the beheading itself are far more incredible. When Alban and his captors are unable to cross a bridge because of crowds, the saint parted the river like Moses. This miracle led to the conversion of his executioner, who joined Alban in martyrdom. But the substitute executioner, Bede says, was not allowed to rejoice in his duty: 'As the martyr's head fell, [the executioner's] eyes dropped out onto the ground.'

Alban became Britain's first recorded martyr, but by no means the only one. Even Bede reports that two Christians from Caerleon-upon-Usk, Aaron and Julius, were martyred during the same persecution.

From division, unity

Not all Christians went so willingly to their deaths. In North Africa, reluctance towards martyrdom led to a permanent split in the church. In 311, 80 North African bishops opposed the ordination of Caecilian as bishop of Carthage. It was not that Caecilian had done anything

'For Christ's sake, [Alban] bore the most horrible torments patiently and gladly, and... the judge saw that no torture could break him or make him renounce the worship of Christ...'

BEDE,
*A HISTORY OF THE
ENGLISH CHURCH
AND PEOPLE*

The half-converts

Although syncretistic beliefs have been overemphasized by recent writers wanting to show Celtic Christianity as practically pagan, there are several surviving artefacts demonstrating that early conversion could be slow. Pagans and Christians apparently both worshipped in the same building at Lullingstone, Kent. Other early Christian churches in Britain seem to have been built in deliberate imitation of pagan Roman temples and shrines. Meanwhile, a mosaic discovered in Hinton Mary, Dorset, incorporates several pagan and Christian themes. Such is also the case in Ireland, where pagan and Christian statues were found side by side.

wrong – but the bishop who ordained him had, in their minds. During Diocletian's Great Persecution, this bishop had handed over sacred Christian works to his oppressors to avoid death. The embittered North African bishops (led by Donatus, and thus called Donatists) appointed someone else for the position. Who, then, was the real bishop of Carthage? And could those who had lapsed under persecution ever again be considered real Christians? 'The servants of God are those who are hated by the world,' claimed the Donatists. Augustine of Hippo spoke for the moderates among the North African church leadership: 'The clouds roll with thunder that the House of the Lord shall be built throughout the earth; and these frogs sit in the marshes and croak, "We are the only Christians!"'

Both sides appealed to Emperor Constantine, credited with establishing religious freedom and promoting Christianity. Under his auspices, in AD 314 bishops came to the southern Gaul city of Arles from around the Christian world to discuss the Carthage controversy. Not only did they declare Caecilian the true bishop of the city, but they pronounced the Donatists heretics. ('What has the emperor to do with the church?' the Donatists huffed, and continued a schism that lasted until the Muslims invaded North Africa in the 8th century.) Meanwhile, the bishops decided that as long as they were in Arles, they might as well take care of other matters. Gladiators, circus charioteers and theatre workers were excommunicated. Ministers were ordered to stay in the place where they were ordained. Furthermore, in a move that would later become important for the Celtic churches, Pope Sylvester was asked to decide how to determine Easter, 'so that it may be celebrated by us on the same day and at the same time throughout the whole church'.

Among the signatories of these 22 canons were three bishops from Britain: Eborius of York, Restitutus of London and Adelphius of Lincoln. Two others, a presbyter named Sacerdus and a deacon named Arminius, were also from Britain. The numbers may seem small, considering that only five signatories came from the island, but they do not necessarily mean that the British church was tiny. We know that Gaul had 36 bishops at the time, but only 16 attended the Council of Arles. It would have been even more difficult for British bishops to make their way to the city. Nevertheless, British bishops made it not only to Arles in 314, but to the councils of Sardica (Sophia) in 343 and Armininum (Rimini) in 359. At the latter of these, the emperor offered to pay the expenses of all the bishops from Gaul and Britain. Only three British bishops accepted, noting that they were short of cash and did not want to impose on church friends.

That the British church was able to join in so many church councils not only suggests that they were organized relatively early – certainly before Constantine's Edict of Milan granted religious freedom – but also demonstrates that they had extensive contact with the church in North Africa, continental Europe and elsewhere. It was from North Africa that an idea sprang that would resonate through the entire Celtic world – monasticism.

Green deserts

Isolation in the sandy wastelands of the Middle East had always held a special kind of spiritual importance. God spoke to Moses alone on Mount Sinai; Jesus spent 40 days in the Judean wilderness before beginning his public ministry; John the Baptist lived off locusts and honey while residing in the desert. But Antony (251–356), an Egyptian who began a radical existence of poverty and isolation, set the monastic example for centuries. Many disciples sought him out in the Egyptian desert, but thousands more would follow his lead when Athanasius, one of the greatest theologians of the early church, wrote his biography.

The tales of Antony and the other Desert Fathers were promoted heavily by Martin of Tours, a pagan-born ex-soldier from what is now Hungary. Like many other well-known Christian heroes, Martin regularly vacillated between monasticism and church administration, but he was also heavily involved in evangelism. He helped to establish the first monastery in Gaul (at Ligugé), but also made many missionary trips through the countryside, promoting Christianity to the heathen and monasticism to the already converted. One of these Christians who reportedly accepted Martin's call was Ninian, a Briton.

The tale of Ninian, like many characters from church history, is shadowy and unclear. We cannot even be sure of his name: Thomas Clancy of Glasgow University's Celtic department recently made headlines claiming that Bede mispelled Ninian's real name, Uinniau. 'There are quite a lot of stories from the Middle Ages about St Ninia, as he was then called,' Clancy told *The Times* of London. 'But before that time there is nothing written in history to suggest that he existed. There is no mention about cults or churches, which you would expect if he had been so prominent. We do, however, have evidence of St Uinniau, who was in the same area as the so-called St Ninian at the same time. So it appears there has been a mix-up.'

No one knows where Ninian's Candida Casa stood, but some claim the ruins of this 13th-century chapel stand on the site.

In any case, Ninian (or Uinniau) is credited with being a missionary to Scotland's Picts. He was not necessarily the first to take the gospel north of Hadrian's wall, but he is the first to get credit for it. Martin of Tours reportedly encouraged a few masons to accompany Ninian, and they built a stone church in what is now Whithorn. Bede says it was named Candida Casa, the white house, because the locals had never seen such a structure before.

According to Ninian's unreliable biographer, Aelred (who wrote more to promote Whithorn's authority over

The 6th-century
Caldey stone is
inscribed in both
Latin and Ogham
(note the ridges
at the top left).

other monasteries than to accurately tell the saint's story), the evangelist was so blessed by God in his Christian studies that he did not even need the Candida Casa for shelter. 'When everything around him was soaked, he sat alone with his little book in the downpour, as if protected by the roof of a house,' Aelred wrote. Only once did God's unseen umbrella fail – when 'an unlawful thought stirred in him and desire [was] prompted by the devil'. Drenched and discovered, Ninian 'blushed that he had been overtaken by a vain thought, and in the same moment of time drove away the thought and stayed the shower'.

Ninian's Candida Casa became a monastic centre, eventually drawing students from Ireland and Wales. Ninian, too, made sure to find solitude apart from his administrative tasks and evangelistic work. The cave in which he reportedly took frequent refuge can still be seen today. Its walls have been worn smooth by centuries of waves, but a cross, carved by later disciples, is said to remain.

But as the Picts put pressure on the Roman armies from the north, the heart of the empire itself was facing attack from Germanic tribes. Needing military strength to defend the empire rather than to extend it, Emperor Honorius in 407 recalled the soldiers in Britain to Italy. Within a few years, Roman rule of the island had been obliterated, and within a generation almost all traces of Roman culture – from religion to aqueducts – had vanished. But the withdrawal of Roman troops left the Britons open to invasions from elsewhere. The Picts descended and Scots invaded from Ireland. The real societal change, however, came when Saxons invaded from Germany, followed by Angles, and Jutes from Denmark. The foreign cultures overtook Britain, extinguishing the vestiges of Roman culture; in the eastern parts of the island, Celtic culture disappeared too.

Swords alone did not 'Anglicize' (and Saxonize) the

*'Resolute,
sometimes
impetuous, and
often driven to
extremes of
devotion and
self-sacrifice,
[early British
saints] were
great lovers
of God and
neighbour,
at least those
who left them
in peace.'*

RICHARD J. WOODS,
*THE SPIRITUALITY OF
THE CELTIC SAINTS*

Britons. The British aristocrats who had Romanized themselves probably 'Germanized' themselves to maintain their high social status. Immigration, not just battle deaths, changed the country's demographics. But plenty of Britons still inhabited 5th-century Britain. Without Roman infrastructure, however, life had changed. Communication with the continent contracted. With less contact from Rome, British churches became more insular. Past historians have overemphasized the isolation of the British church, suggesting that it developed in a complete vacuum. This is not true – communication between Britain and the rest of the Western church continued throughout its development. But some modern historians take this too far, denying any detachment. The British church did face isolation; and for the monks following in the steps of St Antony and the Desert Fathers of North Africa, isolation was just fine. Monasticism boomed after the withdrawal of Roman armies. Ironically, these monasteries quickly became the centres of ecclesiastic energy. From the end of the 5th century, nearly every British saint remembered today had been a monk at some point during his life.

Saints of the Round Table

While eastern Britain became strongly Anglo-Saxon, western Britain's character was still dominantly Celtic. Most of the lands now known as Wales had been less Romanized than the east, and many managed to hold the Anglo-Saxons at bay for centuries. The most famous name associated with these battles, of course, is Arthur. 'Arthur fought against them in those days with the kings of the Britons but he himself was leader of battles,' says Nennius's 9th-century *Historia Brittonum* (*History of the Britons*), 'And in all the battles he stood forth as victor.' The most famous king of all legends probably really existed as a Celtic chief, and his fame had spread early. *The Gododin*, written about AD 600, trumpets a military leader who 'gorged black ravens' on the corpses of his fallen adversaries, but cedes 'he was no Arthur'. Likely the real Arthur was no Arthur of legend, either. Nevertheless, he is central to many medieval Celtic tales – and makes appearances in the biographies of many Celtic saints.

One of these Arthurian saints is Dubricus, also known as Dyfrig, who is said to have crowned Arthur and is called by Tennyson's *Idylls of the King* 'chief of the church in Britain'. His colleague, Illtud, supposedly served as a knight in Arthur's army. According to one account, Illtud (450–535) may have even been the famed Galahad. Another says Illtud was Arthur's cousin. But Arthurian legends aside, Dubricus and Illtud were well-known in their own rights. The *Life of Samson*, written in about AD 600, calls Illtud 'the most learned of the Britons in both Testaments and in all kinds of knowledge', from geometry to rhetoric. 'And by birth he was a wise magician, having knowledge of the future,' the biographer adds. Originally from Letavi (which is either in Brittany or central Brednock, England), Illtud is said to have spent his military days a married man – until an angel appeared and urged him to forsake wife and weapons to become a monk. He did so, and around the year 500 founded a church, monastery and school by the Bristol Channel at what is now Llantwit Major in Glamorgan. Its

Peter Langtoft's *Anglo-Norman Chronicle*, published in 1307, hails Arthur as the greatest of kings.

original name came from its founder – Llanilltud Fawr (a *llan* is an enclosure). There he led many disciples in such spiritual devotions as *laus perennis* – unceasing praise. The community's 24 groups were each responsible for an hour of prayer each day. Illtud also kept his mind focused on earth – quite literally. He created new methods of irrigation and cultivation, and even provided other monasteries with his excess seeds. His ex-wife, meanwhile, apparently took the rejection in her stride – who can argue with an angel? – and reportedly founded her own oratory nearby for nuns and widows.

One of Illtud's most famous students was Samson (c. 485–565), a Welshman who had a penchant for wandering – and for succeeding unlucky abbots. After his tutelage under Illtud, Samson went to Ynys Byr (Caldey Island). Not long after his arrival, the *Life of Samson* recounts, tragedy struck:

One dark night, [the abbot] took a solitary stroll into the grounds of the monastery, and what is more serious, so it is said, owing to stupid intoxication, fell headlong into a deep pit. Uttering one piercing cry for help, he was dragged out of the hole by the brothers in a dying condition, and died in the night from his adventure.

Samson was made abbot, and, notes his biographer, 'nobody ever saw him drunk... not even in the least degree did any kind of drink injure him in any way'.

Before long, Samson left Ynys Byr to accept an invitation by Irish monks to visit their abbey. Attempting to return to Britain, Samson was stopped by another monk. 'The devil has possessed our abbot,' he explained. Could Samson help? He could, and did. 'While St Samson prayed, the possessed one, in his bed, by God's help, recovered his reason... gave his monastery with all its substance to Samson and... followed St Samson to this side of the sea and was always his companion,' says the *Life of Samson* (which may be the earliest biography of a

British saint). 'Of his good deeds and good conversation after his fall I know full well, but his name I do not know.'

The monk's long résumé continues. Returning to Britain, he set up an oratory, but a synod commanded him to become abbot of Llantwit Major. Not long afterward, an angel told him, 'Thou oughtest to tarry no longer in this country, for thou art ordained to be a pilgrim, and beyond the sea thou wilt be very great in the Church and worthy of the highest priestly dignity.' So off he went to Cornwall, founding four monasteries (installing his father as abbot of one of them). Cornwall could not hold him, either – from there he crossed to Brittany, founding more monasteries. With such an itinerant life, it is hard to place Samson in any 'hometown', but one of these Brittany monasteries managed to make it stick: he is now known as Samson of Dol.

David of Wales

No saint is now more associated with Wales than David (Dewi in his native language). Another reputed student of Illtud, David was reportedly destined for spiritual greatness even before his birth (but then again, the stories of many saints are full of miracles *in utero*). His life had an unfortunate beginning: his mother, a nun named Non, was raped by a local prince. The impregnated Non, however, was honoured, not scorned. As the story goes, when the pregnant Non entered a local church, the priest was immediately struck dumb; because David would surpass all other preachers, God miraculously forbade his inferiors to lecture in his presence.

David is also credited with founding 12 monasteries, though many of these claims are questionable (including Glastonbury). He is more assuredly associated with the founding of Mynyw, which he named for his hometown and is now called St David's. Here he gained fame as a

'The whole of his day [David] spent, inflexibly and unweariedly, in teaching, praying, genuflecting, and in care of his brethren. He also fed a multitude of orphans, wards, widows, needy, sick, feeble, and pilgrims. Thus he began; thus he continued; thus he ended his day.'

RHIGYFARCH, *LIFE OF DAVID*

radical ascetic, with discipline and severity intentionally rivalling Antony's successors in Egypt. 'He imitated the monks of Egypt and lived a life like theirs,' says his biographer. But where the North African monks focused their asceticism on the rocks and sands, David's focus – water – was more suited to his island life. His nickname, Aquaticus (the Waterman) is mostly due to his requiring total abstinence from alcohol. Other aspects of his life were water-oriented as well. The only condoned meat was fish (bread and vegetables were also allowed). And each day, after morning prayers, David 'plunged himself into cold water, remaining in it sufficiently long to subdue all the ardors of the flesh'. David's unreliable

David's opposition

The foundation of one of David's early monasteries was not appreciated by one of the local men, says the hagiographer Rhigyfarch. But Baia's wife was even more angry, telling her husband 'Rise up… and with swords drawn attack these men who have dared to do such a wicked thing and kill them all.' Baia and his men went out to do just that, but changed their minds along the way. Baia's wife then decided to take the situation into her own hands, telling her maids to run around naked in front of the monks, 'using crude words'. They did so, 'imitating sexual intercourse and displaying love's seductive embraces', says Rhigyfarch. 'They drew the minds of some of the monks towards desire, while to others they were an annoyance.' When the monks decided to give up and leave the area, David told them to stay: 'Be strong and invincible in the struggle, in case your enemy should rejoice in your flight.' Rhigyfarch, meanwhile, rejoiced in the destruction of David's enemies. Baia, he says, was 'struck down by an enemy who took him by surprise', while his wife went mad, killed her stepdaughter, and disappeared forever.

hagiographer, Rhigyfarch, even says the saint 'changed the foul water to healthy' at Bath, 'endowing it with a continuous heat that made it suitable for bathing'. David's rule was apparently among the harshest in Britain. No animals were used in ploughing. 'Every man his own ox,' David mandated. Personal property was outlawed. 'Whoever should say "my book" or "my anything else" was immediately subject to a severe penance,' says Rhigyfarch. New candidates for the monastery had to enter 'naked, as though from a shipwreck', and had to wait at the monastery's door for ten days before even being considered. Despite all of this, says Rhigyfarch, 'No complaint was heard; in

St David's Cathedral, which sits on the old monastery site, was one of the most popular pilgrimage sites of the Middle Ages. Two trips here equalled one to Rome.

fact, there was no conversation beyond that which was necessary.'

All that glitters in the 'golden age of saints'...

Such austerity scandalized Gildas (c. 497–570), an angry saint who is credited as one of Britain's first historians. Ploughing without an ox was a likely sign of presumption and pride, he wrote. Where rules like David's penalized indulgences in worldly pleasures, Gildas penalized abstinence without charity. And where extreme ascetics sought isolation, Gildas outlawed leaving a monastic community for a more solitary devotional life. Reclusive monks, however, were only a small part of the problem in the eye of Gildas, born on the banks of the Clyde in Scotland and educated under Illtud at Llantwit Major. For him, the entire country had forsaken God: a case he made in *De excidio et conquestu Britanniae* (*The Ruin and Conquest of Britain*). 'Kings hath Britain, but they are tyrants,' he wrote. 'Judges she hath, but they are impious; priests hath Britain, but they are fools; pastors so-called, but they are wolves alert to slay souls. They do not look to the good of their people, but to the filling of their own

'Holy men used to visit Gildas from distant parts of Britain, and when advised, returned and cherished with delight the encouragements and counsels they had heard from him.'

CARADOC OF
LLANGARFAN,
*THE LIFE OF
GILDAS*, c. 1150

bellies.' It was the fault of these temporal and spiritual rulers, Gildas wrote, that the Anglo-Saxon invaders had met with such success. But even the pagan foreigners could not be blamed with filling both church and state with evil – the lax Britons themselves were responsible for such tragedy. 'God's church and his holy law', he lamented, were mocked by those in power.

About a century and a half before Gildas, another British Christian, probably from Wales, similarly ranted against apathy in the Christian church. But this itinerant preacher and former lawyer railed against a sinful church in Rome, not Britain – and became one of the most famous Western heretics in church history. The life story of Pelagius cannot be told accurately. We do know that he was a layman born around 354 somewhere in the British Isles. One of his chief accusers, Jerome, disparagingly says he was 'stuffed with the porridge of the Scots', and he was regularly referred to as Pelagius Brito, Britannus, and other such names that give historical evidence to his general background, if not hometown. Known as Pelagius to history, he was probably born Morgan (or Morien). In the early 380s he went to Rome to study law, but decided

Steep Holme Island in the Bristol Channel, where Gildas reportedly spent seven years.

upon his arrival to enter full-time ministry ('The world is saved and inheritance and civil suits are plucked from the abyss because this man, neglecting the law courts, has turned to the Church,' Jerome quipped sarcastically.) He was a huge man, perhaps even larger than the six-foot-plus David of Wales. Another critic, in a letter to Pelagius, wrote of his 'broad shoulders and robust neck, showing your fat even on your forehead'. What angered so many church fathers was Pelagius's claims that humans had absolute free will and an inherent capacity to do good. This was at odds with the doctrines of original sin and divine grace articulated by Augustine of Hippo. Pelagius was particularly upset with Augustine's famous prayer, 'Give what Thou commandest and command what Thou wilt.' To Pelagius, such an emphasis had led to the church's lazy morality: If grace was given freely without any nod to merit, what was the use in doing good at all? Even worse in Pelagius's eyes, Augustine denied that sinless perfection was possible, even after baptism! Had not God himself commanded, 'Be perfect, even as I am perfect?'

Under attack from Augustine, Jerome and others, Pelagius was condemned by two African councils in 416, and was excommunicated by Pope Innocent I in 417. But his ideas lived on, especially in Britain. Bede says that British churches were so overwhelmed with Pelagian teachings that they had to send for help from Gaul. The reply came in the form of two men, Germanus of Auxerre and (probably) Lupus of Troyes. *The Chronicle of Prosper of Aquitaine*, a chronological listing of important events in church history, sees the story slightly differently. Its entry for the year 429 says:

Pope Innocent I died shortly after his excommunication of Pelagius. His successor reopened the heretic's case, but eventually agreed with his predecessor.

The Pelagian Agricola... insidiously corrupted the churches of Britain with his teachings. But, through the negotiation of the deacon Palladius, Pope Celestine sent Germanus, Bishop of Auxerre, to act on his behalf, and he routed the heretics and directed the Britons to the Catholic faith.

In the entry for 431, the deacon appears again: 'Palladius was ordained by Pope Celestine and sent to the Irish believers in Christ as their first bishop.'

C H A P T E R   3

Patrick and the Conversion of Ireland

P alladius's appearance as the bishop of Irish Christians in Prosper's reliable *Chronicle* raises more questions than it answers. Where did these Irish Christians come from? How many were there? How had they been converted? For later writers attempting to support the idea of Patrick as apostle of Ireland, there were even bigger problems. How could Patrick be credited with converting the island if Palladius had got there first? Muirchú moccu Machteni, who wrote an unreliable hagiography of Patrick around 695, had an answer. 'No one can receive from earth what has not been given by heaven: Palladius was denied success,' he wrote. 'For these wild and obdurate people did not readily accept his doctrine and he himself did not wish to spend a long time in a foreign country, but to return to him who had sent him.'

Palladius's return journey, however, ended on the other side of the Irish Sea – he died almost immediately after leaving Ireland. (Other unreliable accounts say Palladius was martyred by the Irish.) Patrick then swooped in a year later and saved the day – and the island. Why a year later? In the hagiographies, Patrick had to arrive after Palladius, lest Rome's initiative and apostolic authority be deprecated. But Patrick's mission could not seem too long after that of Palladius – others could stake claims as missionaries to at least part of the island. Muirchú wanted Patrick to be apostle of all Ireland – not just some of it. Therefore, because of the hagiographer's efforts, 432 is in the history books as the start of Patrick's mission. (At least that is the current theory. Who knows? Maybe Muirchú actually had information about Palladius's work.) The reality is that we have no idea on the specifics of when Patrick actually went to Ireland, when and where he was born, where he lived and worked, when and where he died, or any of the other important historical reference points. There are some historical clues that help, however, including language. For example, it is clear by examining the way certain Latin words were integrated into the Irish language that Christianity came from Britain, not continental Europe. In addition to such detective work, we also have historical gold – two works undoubtedly written by Patrick himself – one of them outlining his life story.

While we have a story without specifics for Patrick, in Palladius we have specifics without a story. Unlike Patrick, Palladius has no extant writings describing his motivation, his fears, or his concerns. But while modern historians have rejected the explanations of Muirchú and others, they have come up with their own theories of Palladius's internal life. The picture that emerges is that Pope Celestine – and thus his deacon – had two main priorities in Ireland: countering Pelagianism and extending the Roman church. After Emperor Honorius exiled all Pelagians on 30 April 418, the Pelagians simply retreated beyond the reach of the Roman empire, to Britain. Palladius probably wanted to make sure that if Pelagians were banished from Britain (Germanus's job), they did not simply retreat again to Ireland. Extending the church to the furthest reaches of the known world was also a matter of both spiritual and political significance. As one historian recently wrote:

The activities of Germanus and Palladius, in Britain and in Ireland, demonstrated that a Christian and papal Rome, the Rome of Peter and Paul [as opposed to that of Romulus and Remus], could intervene to safeguard and to spread the

'When I came to Patrick, I found it impossible to gain any clear conception of the man and his work. The subject was wrapt in obscurity, and this obscurity was encircled in an atmosphere of controversy and conjecture.'

J.B. BURY,
*THE LIFE OF
ST PATRICK AND
HIS PLACE IN
HISTORY,* 1905

*Faith in an island which had thrown off imperial authority
and also in another island which had never been subject to
the sway of the emperor.*

Extending its reach not only enhanced the pope's claims
to superiority over the church, but also over the state.

So if Palladius was so important to the church, what
happened? Where are his hagiographies? Where are his
stories? It is very possible they still exist to this day –
only now many of the stories of Palladius are attributed
to Patrick.

From slave to saint

Today, Patrick is arguably the most famous saint from
the 5th century. Each year, when parades in New York,
Boston and elsewhere celebrate in his name, a few stories
are brought out and passed around again: Patrick drove
the snakes out of Ireland; he used the shamrock to
explain the Trinity; he single-handedly converted the
entire country – without a drop of blood; he offered 'the
first de-Romanized Christianity in human history'. Pity
that none of these common beliefs about Patrick can be
justified by reliable texts.

Patrick was born into an apparently affluent,
religious home. His father, Calpornius, was a deacon,
and his grandfather, Potitus, had been a priest. The
family was probably part of the local nobility, and owned,
in Patrick's words, a 'small estate near the village of
Bannavem Taburniae'. (The exact location of this town,
which may have been called Banneventa Burniae, is a
matter of regular dispute. Because of the uncertainly,
dozens of sites along the shores of western Britain claim
to be Patrick's hometown.) As noted earlier, being part of
the local nobility (*civitas*) in the 400s had its benefits and
perils. Wealth and power made life comfortable – but they
also made one a target; and there were no more Roman
soldiers for protection. Patrick learned this first-hand in a
rather unfortunate way – at the age of 16, he was captured

*'The Irish gave
Patrick more
than a home –
they gave him a
role, a meaning
to his life. For
only this former
slave had the
right instincts
to impart to the
Irish a New
Story, one that
made new sense
of all their old
stories and
brought them a
peace they had
never known
before.'*

THOMAS CAHILL,
*HOW THE IRISH
SAVED CIVILIZATION*

by Irish slave-raiders and taken across the sea into captivity.

Patrick says little about his life and the master he served for the next six years of his life, except to say that he 'was made to shepherd the flocks day after day'. The unreliable Tírechán, a 7th-century bishop, says his owner's name was Mílluc moccu Bóin (Milchu), a druid. 'Patrick worked for him in every kind of servitude and heavy labour, and Mílluc placed him as a swineherd in the mountain glens,' he wrote. Herding animals can be a rough and lonely life. Patrick reportedly endured long bouts of hunger, thirst and isolation in the Irish hills. It was during this time that he turned to the Christian God of his family for comfort.

Decades later, writing his *Confessio*, Patrick believed that his slavery was God's punishment for religious apathy. 'I was taken into captivity in Ireland – at that time I was ignorant of the true God – along with many thousand others,' he wrote. 'This was our punishment for departing from God, abandoning his commandments, and ignoring our priests who kept on warning us about our salvation.' The punishment was also grace, and during his captivity Patrick found God:

More and more, the love of God and the fear of him grew in me, and my faith was increased and my spirit enlivened. So much that I prayed up to a hundred times in the day, and almost as often at night. I even remained in the wood and on the mountain to pray. And – come hail, rain, or snow – I was up before dawn to pray, and I sensed no evil nor spiritual laziness within.

He may have enjoyed making himself a slave to Christ, but Patrick was less inclined to remain a slave to Mílluc. At age 22, he heard a supernatural voice. 'You do well to fast,' the voice said. 'Soon you will return to your homeland.' The voice soon spoke again: 'Behold! Your ship is prepared.' The only problem was that the ship had been

'He [Patrick] conquered by steadfastness of faith, by glowing zeal, and by the attractive power of love.'

AUGUST NEANDER, *GENERAL HISTORY OF THE CHRISTIAN RELIGION AND CHURCH*, 1855

God called him'. More likely are reports that Patrick travelled to Gaul, where he studied under Germanus of Auxerre, the anti-Pelagian bishop Pope Celestine sent to Britain. Here Muirchú gets cloudy, which is ironically a sign that he might be more accurate: 'some say he spent forty years there', the hagiographer writes, 'some say thirty'.

Just before Patrick was ordained as a deacon, he confessed a sin to his closest friend. There is no way of knowing what the sin was, but it was probably serious – he had committed it around age 15 (about a year before the Irish raiders captured him) and it still bothered him many years later. Some have supposed that the sin was murder,

but it is only a guess. Patrick's *Confessio* tells the story of his confession, but does not repeat it: 'When I was anxious and worried I hinted to my dearest friend about something I had done one day – indeed in one hour – in my youth, for I had not then prevailed over my sinfulness.' His friend did not think it too serious a matter, and forgave him. Certainly he did not think it prohibited him from becoming a deacon. On the contrary, he said, 'Mark my words, you are going to be made bishop.'

In this 13th-century image, Patrick sleeps, watched by Christ.

Patrick said he was unworthy for such a position, but soon attained the rank. His confession to his friend would later come back to haunt him.

While there had to be some Christians in Ireland – who else would have asked Celestine to send a bishop? – Patrick apparently did not encounter them when he returned. 'I dwell among gentiles, in the midst of pagan barbarians, worshippers of idols, and of unclean things,' he wrote. But he maintains he was changing all that. 'In Ireland… they never had knowledge of God and celebrated only idols and unclean things,' he wrote. 'Until now.'

In both his surviving works, Patrick portrays himself humbly. 'I am the sinner Patrick,' he begins the *Confessio*.

'I am the most unsophisticated of people, the least
of Christians, and for many people I am the most
contemptible… It is among the people of [Ireland] that
my smallness is seen.' Most of this, however, was probably
rhetorical humility, like the apostle Paul's statements
that he is 'the least of Christians' (Ephesians 3:8) and the
'chief of sinners' (1 Timothy 1:15). Patrick actually saw his
work as crucial to the work of the church. Not only was he
literally fulfilling Jesus' command to tell people about him
'to the ends of the earth' (Acts 1:8), but by doing so he was
hastening Christ's return.

At the end of the world

Surviving maps by Ptolemy (a 2nd-century astronomer,
mathematician and geographer from Alexandria) and
from a 13th-century copy of the book of Psalms have
significant differences. In the latter, Jerusalem is the
centre of the world, and Christ oversees all. But in both
maps, Ireland (Hibernia) is practically unseen – it is so
far on the margins that it is practically falling off. Such
geography was firmly established in Patrick's mind as
well. 'Truly, I am greatly in God's debt,' he wrote:

*He has given me a great grace, that through me many
peoples might be reborn and later brought to completion;
and that from among them everywhere clerics should be
ordained [to serve] this people – who have but recently
come to belief – [and] which the Lord has taken [to himself]
'from the ends of the earth'. He thus fulfilled 'what he once
promised through his prophets': 'to you shall the nations
come from the ends of the earth and say, "Our fathers have
inherited naught but lies, worthless things in which there
is no profit" [Jeremiah 16:19]'. And in another place: 'I have
set you to be a light for the nations, that you may bring
salvation to the uttermost parts of the earth.'*

In Patrick's mind, preaching at the end of the world
meant bringing about the end of the world. He repeatedly

*'I was like a
stone lying in
the deepest
mire; and then,
"he who is
mighty" came,
and, in his
mercy, raised
me up. He most
truly raised me
on high and
set me on top
of the rampart.'*

PATRICK,
CONFESSIO

mentions that he is in 'the last days', and regularly quotes Jesus' words in Matthew 24:14: 'All nations will hear the gospel, and then, finally, the end will come.' 'And this is what we see,' Patrick writes. 'It has been fulfilled. Behold! We are [now] witnesses to the fact that the gospel has been preached out to beyond where anyone lives.'

Scholars in the late 15th century recreated the map of Greek astronomer Ptolemy (c. 100–68) by using data from his work *Geography*. In both time periods, Ireland was seen as at the edges of the known world.

Patrick was not alone in this belief. Christians never gave up the idea that Christ would return when all the nations heard about him; they simply discovered more nations. A millennium after Patrick, Columbus would be driven to America not merely in a quest of fame and riches, but to hasten the Second Coming. 'God made me

the messenger of the New Heaven and the New Earth,' he wrote. Columbus even penned his own *Book of Prophesies* to show how his discovery fitted into biblical predictions. In fact, the belief continues today; the major missions push of the late 20th century, with its emphasis on 'unreached people groups', was largely based in the promise of Matthew 24:14.

Rejecting gods of three for the Trinity

Little is known of Patrick's specific conversion methods. The tale about his using a shamrock to explain the Trinity is almost certainly untrue. It would have been unnecessary. A common theme throughout Celtic religion is triune gods – gods with three manifestations, gods who travel in threes, or gods with three heads.

We know this about pagan Celtic religion partly through archaeology, but also because later Celtic scribes believed, like Patrick, that pagan religions were pre-Christian rather than anti-Christian. Early and medieval Christians believed Paul's words that 'ever since the creation of the world, God's eternal power and divine nature, invisible though they are, have been understood and are seen through the things he has made' (Romans 1:20). Paul himself exemplified this belief in Athens. He was 'deeply distressed to see that the city was full of idols', but used them in evangelism. 'I see how extremely religious you are in every way,' Paul told the Athenians. 'I found an altar with the inscription, "To an unknown god". What therefore you worship as unknown, this I proclaim to you' (Acts 17:16ff.). Pagan beliefs were therefore part of the 'eternity written

Celtic gods were often depicted with three faces, as in this life-size stone carving from the 2nd century BC.

on the hearts' of those who never had the chance to hear
the full truth.

This is not to say that Patrick and his contemporaries
in any way approved of paganism as a distant relative to
their religion. On the contrary, they believed that the pagan
gods and other supernatural beings likely did exist, but were
demons. The old pagan stories did not have to be expelled,
they only had to be reinterpreted. Miracles, magic and
mysteries probably did occur, the Christians reasoned. Even
Pharaoh's magicians had powers – but the God of Moses
was more powerful, and more importantly, he was good.

The druids 'wished to kill holy Patrick', the
hagiographies tell us over and over again. These claims
cannot be wholly dismissed. Patrick and other missionaries
almost certainly faced opposition from the druids – not
simply because they were the religious leaders but because
they had the most to lose if the culture converted. Indeed,
that is what happened – the church replaced the druids as
the hub of society. Patrick confirmed that his life was in
danger. 'Daily I expect murder, fraud, or captivity,' he wrote.
'But I fear none of these things because of the promises of
heaven. I have cast myself into the hands of God almighty
who rules everywhere.' (But while he cast himself into the
hands of God, he also cast protection money into the hands
of his would-be enemies. 'Patrick paid the price of 15 souls
in gold and silver so that no evil persons should impede
them as they travelled straight across the whole of Ireland,'
one hagiographer wrote. In the *Confessio*, Patrick proudly
admits paying 15 judges 'so that you might enjoy me and I
might always enjoy you in God'.)

Patrick does not record any confrontations with
druids, but it is the subject of one of the most famous
stories of his life. Since Muirchú is our source, it is likely
not a word of it is true. The night before Easter reportedly
happened to coincide with a major pagan festival on the
Hill of Tara. In defiance of pagan tradition, Patrick lit a
bonfire in the distance – but in full view of King Loiguire.
'Who is it who has dared to commit this crime in my

*'A capacity for
worship, a
passionate
feeling for the
supernatural,
for the gods, or
later, God, is,
I believe, the
truest and most
binding cultural
element
throughout the
entire Celtic
world.'*

ANNE ROSS,
*PAGAN CELTIC
BRITAIN*

kingdom?' the king asked. 'He must die.' The king sent several men – including druids – to seize the missionary. Brought before the king, Patrick was anything but passive. He summoned the power of God to raise one of the druids into the air, then released him. 'Coming down, he smashed his skull on a rock, and died right before them; and the heathen were afraid,' Muirchú says. Then Patrick called down darkness and an earthquake. 'By this disaster, caused by Patrick's curse in the king's presence because of the king's order, seven times seven men fell.'

The next day, Easter Sunday, Patrick entered Loiguire's banquet hall. A druid challenged him to a wonder-working battle. First the druid made snow fall waist-deep. Patrick made it disappear. Then the druid made fog over the land. Patrick cleared it away, too. Then, in a final test, the prayers of Patrick set the druid ablaze. When the enraged king started at Patrick, the missionary stopped him, saying, 'If you do not believe now, you will die on the spot; for the wrath of God descends on your head.'

'It is better for me to believe than to die,' Loiguire reasoned. Adds Muirchú, 'He believed on that day and turned to the eternal Lord God. Many others also believed on that day.'

Most historians dismiss the tale as a retelling of Moses' encounter with Pharaoh's magicians or Elijah's encounter with the prophets of Baal on Mount Carmel. But to Patrick and his contemporaries, such comparisons would not be evidence of Muirchú's plagiarism. It would have been evidence of God's consistency.

If the hagiographers present Patrick's evangelism methods as unrelenting and deadly, they also present them as gentle and graceful. Tírechán's account of the conversion of Loiguire's daughters is lovely, if implausible in its details. 'Who is God, and where is God, and whose God is he, and where is his house?' one of the women asked Patrick. 'Give us some idea of him: how he may be seen, how loved; how he may be found.'

'Our God is the God of all people,' Patrick replied:

'Hear all ye who love God, the holy merits of the Bishop Patrick, a man blessed in Christ; how, on account of his good actions, he is likened unto the angels, and for his perfect life, is counted equal to the apostles.'

HYMN OF
ST PATRICK,
ATTRIBUTED TO
SECUNDINUS

The God of heaven and earth, of the sea and of the rivers, the God of the sun and the moon and of all the stars, the God of the high mountains and of the deep valleys. He is God above heaven and in heaven and under heaven, and has as his dwelling place heaven and earth and the sea and all that are in them. His life is in all things; he makes all things live; he governs all things; he supports all things… Truly now, since you are daughters of an earthly king, I wish that you will believe and I wish to wed you to the king of heaven.

They agreed and were baptized. Then they immediately died, their souls ascending to heaven. It is not exactly the modern happy ending, but it apparently suited Tírechán.

Prayer of protection

Patrick's most famous work almost certainly was not written by him. The *Lorica* (or Breastplate), also known as 'The Deer's Cry' because it supposedly helped him change into the shape of a deer when Loiguire hunted him, was probably first written in the 7th or 8th century. 'I rise today', it begins, 'in the power's strength, invoking the Trinity, believing in threeness, confessing the oneness, of creation's Creator…'

I rise today with the power of God to pilot me, God's strength to sustain me, God's wisdom to guide me, God's eye to look ahead for me, God's ear to hear me, God's word to speak for me, God's hand to protect me, God's way to defend me, God's host to deliver me from snares of devils, from evil temptations, from nature's failings, from all who wish to harm me, far or near, alone and in a crowd…

Christ with me, Christ before me, Christ behind me; Christ within me, Christ beneath me, Christ above me; Christ in my lying, Christ in my sitting, Christ in my rising; Christ in the heart of all who think of me, Christ on the tongue of all who speak to me, Christ in the eye of all who see me, Christ in the ear of all who hear me… May your salvation, Lord, be with us always.

There may be a hint of truth behind this story. 'The Irish leaders' sons and daughters are seen to become the monks and virgins of Christ,' Patrick writes in the *Confessio*. And again in his *Letter to Coroticus*: 'Indeed, I could not count how many of the sons and daughters of the rulers of the Irish had become monks and virgins of Christ.' Patrick apparently acted as a foster-parent to many rulers' children. This was an old Irish custom and one of the main societal bonds at the time. In most cases, the natural parents gave the foster parents an 'after-gift'. In Patrick's case, money seems to have gone the other direction. No matter for Patrick – the true value lay in bringing more souls to conversion.

Patrick the abolitionist

Patrick was very protective of his converts, and it is because of his defence of them that we have his other document, the *Letter to the Soldiers of Coroticus*. It addresses an intimately familiar enemy – slavery. Its target is Coroticus, a Christian tyrant from Britain who had captured many of Patrick's converts the day after their baptism. 'Still wearing their white baptismal garb [and with] the chrism still on their foreheads,' the young Irish Christians were 'cut down and cruelly put to the sword by these men', Patrick raged. 'Ravenous wolves have gulped down the Lord's own flock which was flourishing in Ireland and the whole church cries out and laments for its sons and daughters.'

The *Letter to the Soldiers of Coroticus* is not just a letter to the soldiers of Coroticus – it is written to 'everyone who fears God'. Patrick's correspondence is designed to excommunicate the slave raiders and their leader. 'The soldiers of Coroticus are strangers to me and to Christ, my God,' he wrote. 'It is not lawful to seek favour from men such as these, nor to eat food or drink with them; nor to accept their alms until they make satisfaction to God with painful penance and the shedding of tears, and free the baptized servants of God.'

Whether Patrick's letter worked or if the slaves were

freed is unknown. Muirchú claims Coroticus laughed at the epistle, but Patrick and his God took vengeance. Before the eyes of his closest followers, the tyrant was magically 'transformed into the shape of a little fox' and ran away, never to be seen again.

Patrick had to spend much of his *Letter to the Soldiers of Coroticus* explaining that he was not exceeding his jurisdiction by excommunicating the raiders. If Coroticus was indeed British, then explanation was probably necessary – especially if Patrick was already in trouble with the British church leadership.

Some time after Patrick became bishop, his closest friend betrayed him. The man who had told him, 'Mark my words, you are going to be made bishop', spilled the evangelist's deepest, darkest secret to the church authorities. The disclosure apparently raised quite a scandal – so much so that the church leaders wondered if Patrick could remain a bishop at all. Other charges were added, including one suggesting Patrick had gone to Ireland to financially enrich himself. The church authorities called a synod, and apparently sent a delegation to Ireland to question Patrick. Though Patrick never testified in Britain, his traitorous friend defended him. As the charges circulated on both sides of the Irish Sea, Patrick penned his *Confessio* to refute the charges. All the biographical information he provides serves to defend himself against charges that he had no authority to minister in Ireland, that his conversion tactics were out of order, and that he was enriching himself. God himself had sent him, Patrick asserted, and God was defending him still. 'Indeed he bore me up, though I was trampled underfoot in such a way,' he wrote. 'For although I was put down and shamed, not too much harm came to me.' Though the result is ultimately unclear, Patrick appears to have been successful in his defence.

Beyond the conversion of Ireland

Tradition remembers Patrick as the wandering missionary bishop, converting as much of Ireland as he could before his death. Irish monasticism is more associated with those who came later. But Patrick saw his mission not simply as making Christians – he wanted to make monks and nuns. Like his Christian contemporaries, Patrick saw asceticism as the highest form of the Christian life. He seemed especially proud of a young, beautiful, Irish noblewoman who returned to Patrick a few days after he baptized her, saying 'a divine communication from a messenger of God... advised her to become a virgin of Christ' to become closer to Christ. Though her family opposed her action, six days later she took her vows. The young noblewoman would have become a sister to slaves, who apparently formed a large part of Patrick's nunneries. 'Those held

Croagh Patrick

On 'Reek Sunday', the last Sunday of July, 25,000 or so pilgrims climb (many barefoot) to the top of Croagh Patrick, in County Mayo. The legends say this was where Patrick fasted for 40 days during the Lent of 441, and that this is where he drove the snakes from Ireland. Actually, he did no such thing, but as early as the 1100s Giraldus Cambrensis wrote that no snakes could ever live on the island. 'Sometimes for the sake of experiment serpents have been shipped over,' he wrote, 'but were found lifeless and dead as soon as the middle of the Irish Sea was crossed.'

Whether Patrick actually visited the mountain or not, it has been considered a holy site for a very long time. Carbon dating of an oratory at the 2,710-foot summit puts the church somewhere between AD 430 and 890. In the 1100s, when control of the mountain passed from Armagh to Tuam, the former began promoting its own Patrician pilgrimage point: Patrick's Purgatory, an island supposedly housing a cave where the saint entered the underworld during a period of penance.

in slavery have to work hardest,' Patrick wrote. 'They are continually harassed and even have to suffer being terrorized. But the Lord gives grace to many of his maidservants, and the more they are forbidden to imitate him the more they boldly do this.'

Nobles, slaves, widows and probably even married people (who took a vow of sexual abstinence) joined Patrick's call to the monastic life. If other monasteries made prospects wait outside the door ten days, Patrick apparently ran out the monastery door and pulled potential recruits in with enthusiasm.

Muirchú writes that when Patrick died, 'no night fell; it did not wrap its black wings around the earth; and the

Pilgrims pray atop the 2510-foot Croagh Patrick, known as 'The Reek', where the missionary bishop reportedly fasted.

'Remember St Patrick. Remember what the fidelity of just one man has meant for Ireland and the world.'

POPE JOHN PAUL II,
VISITING IRELAND
IN 1979

evening did not send the darkness which carries the stars. The people of Ulaid say that to the very end of the year in which he departed, the darkness of the nights was never as great as before. There is no doubt that this was testimony to the merit of so great a man.' Muirchú also claims that just before his death, God granted Patrick's demand that he alone shall judge all the Irish, not Christ. In fact, very little can be said with certainty about Patrick's death, except that it almost certainly occurred on 17 March. The year is less certain, though Irish annals place it at 493. Monasteries all over Ireland – including Armagh, Downpatrick and Saul – claim his remains, but they are probably lost forever. A liturgical calendar from 797 remembers him: 'The flame of a splendid sun, the apostle of virgin Erin [Ireland], may Patrick with many thousands be the shelter of our wickedness.' By then, Ireland had been almost totally Christian for two centuries, thanks largely to Patrick.

Ireland's Monks and Monasteries

About the time of Patrick's death, a Pictish warrior-prince named Énda (c. 450–535) was mourning another death – that of his fiancée. His older sister, a nun, told him to stop mourning. After all, she reasoned, all earthly loves eventually expire; only heavenly love lasts forever. Rather than pine for lost love, she said, Énda should follow her into monastic life. The prince agreed, and set off for Ninian's Candida Casa. Years later, he returned to Ireland and around 484 set up a monastery on rocky Inishmore, one of the Aran Islands off western Ireland. According to tradition, his was the first monastery in Ireland.

There are the inevitable challenges to the claim, including the regular caution that the first *known* person

Ruins of the Church of St Benignus, named for Patrick's successor at Armagh, on the island of Inishmore.

to do something often is not the first to actually do it. As noted earlier, Patrick himself urged converts to become monks and nuns, and he may have lived half a century before Énda. The sea has long claimed any ruins of Inishmore's early foundation. Other early monastic settlements, usually made of daub and wattle, have likewise disappeared with time. But more monks and nuns would follow, building foundations throughout Ireland and creating a culture that would become Celtic Christianity's most notable feature.

Some time in the 800s, an unknown writer tried to chart Irish church history from its inception to 665. His *Catalogue of the Saints of Ireland* tells the tale in three stages. Until 544, 350 non-celibate bishops took their lead from Patrick. In the Second Order (544–98), bishops and presbyters shifted their model from Patrick to the ascetic Antony of Egypt, following practices such as 'avoiding the society of women'. The Third Order became most ascetic of all, with monks 'living on herbs and water and from alms'. But the *Catalogue* writer was unlike many of his contemporaries – he believed the trend was a degeneration, not progress. The First Order was 'most holy', the third was merely 'holy'.

Living martyrdom

Actually, Irish monasticism had no such divisible eras. Énda's monastery, for example, was reportedly one of the more austere and demanding of any time. If there was any division seen by the Christian Celts, it was not one of increasingly ascetic ages but one of degrees of self-sacrifice. As one surviving homily, dating from the late 600s or early 700s, says:

There are in fact three kinds of martyrdom, which we may regard as types of cross in human eyes: namely, white martyrdom, green martyrdom, and red martyrdom. A person undergoes white martyrdom when he leaves all for the sake of Christ, even though this means fasting, hunger, and hard work. Green martyrdom is attributed to someone who through them – that is, fasting and work – is freed of his desires, or undergoes travail in sorrow and penance. Red martyrdom is found in the sufferings of a cross of death for Christ's sake, as was the way of the apostles, because of the persecution of the wicked, and while preaching the truths of God.

White martyrdom we will examine more in later chapters. The era of widespread red martyrdom – as experienced by the church in Lyons, Symphorian of Autun and Alban – had abated centuries before the homily was delivered. Green martyrdom, however, would become not just widespread in Ireland – it would become the dominant manifestation of the Irish church. Celtic Christians no longer had death by persecution to guarantee their entrance into heaven, so a metaphorical death, a 'death of desires', became the next best thing. Such practices may have found rich soil in the area where Pelagianism fought Augustine's doctrines of humanity's depravity and God's divine grace. Pelagius had taught that sinless perfection was possible if someone just tried hard enough. And the Celts certainly tried hard to do it. One monk, writing a poem in the 700s or 800s, summarized his lonely life in pursuit of holiness:

All alone in my little cell, without the company of a single person;
precious has been the pilgrimage before going to meet death.
A hidden secluded little hut, for the forgiveness of my sins:
an upright, untroubled conscience towards holy heaven…
A cold and anxious bed, like the lying down of a doomed man:
a brief, apprehensive sleep; invocations frequent and early.
My food as befits my station, precious has been my captivity:
my dinner, without doubt, would not make me full-blooded.
Dry bread weighed out, well we bow the head;
water of the man-coloured hillside, that is the drink I would take.
A bitter meagre dinner; diligently feeding the sick;
keeping off strife and visits; a calm, serene conscience…

'Nowhere in barbarian Europe did monks and their saints so thoroughly dominate the social and spiritual life of the population as in Ireland… Their purpose was at once grand and mundane, selfless and self-serving.'

LISA BITEL,
ISLE OF THE SAINTS

All alone in my little cell, all alone thus;
    alone I came into the world, alone I shall go from it.
If on my own I have sinned through pride of this world,
    hear me wail for it all alone, O God!

Kevin of Glendalough

Two centuries before the poem was written, a recently
ordained monk named Kevin (or Cóemgen) sought such a
holy life in the craggy 'glen of the two lakes' (Glendalough)
in the Wicklow mountains. 'There he had no food but the

The round tower
of Glendalough,
reconstructed
in 1870, stands
watch over the
icy stream where
Kevin used to
bathe in self-
mortification.

nuts of the forest, the herbs of the earth, and fresh water for drinking,' says his hagiographer. 'For sleeping he had only a stone for a pillow.' He spent most of his days and nights reciting prayers in a tiny cave now called 'Kevin's Bed' (only four feet wide, three feet high, and seven feet deep) or waist-deep in the cold lake waters. After seven years of such austerity, he achieved such a reputation for holiness that he began gaining disciples. For their sake, he moved out of the cave and founded the Glendalough monastery. He was a recluse, but apparently not one who

avoided others at all costs – Glendalough was created largely to feed 'companies and strangers and guests and pilgrims… No one was refused entertainment.'

Kevin continued his ascetic life even in the community, maintaining his flagstone bed from his days of isolation and regularly escaping his disciples for intense periods of isolation. In a famous story occurring one Lenten season, Kevin was praying with his arms extended when a blackbird hopped into his hand. He maintained his position so she could build her nest, not moving until after the eggs hatched. As if that was not already an extraordinary story, Kevin's hagiographer claims an angel visited, ordering the saint to put his arms down and return to the monastery. 'It is no great thing for me to bear this pain of holding my hand under the blackbird for the sake of heaven's king, for up on the cross of suffering Jesus bore every pain on behalf of Adam's seed,' Kevin eloquently replied. Other animals feature prominently in his story: an otter brought him a daily salmon and rescued his psalter when it sank to the bottom of the lake.

Meanwhile, Glendalough continued to grow. Hundreds of monks came to the monastery, which added huts to live in, a farm to work on, chapels to pray in, and a school to learn in. The size and shape of monasteries varied widely, from a hermit's hut to a massive settlement. Rules from the 700s, however, indicate how many – especially the large and famous – were laid out: 'four boundaries around a sanctuary, the first into which laymen and women enter, the second into which only clerics come. The first is called holy, the second holier, the third most holy. Note that the name of the fourth is lacking.' The monastic centres were usually circular and enclosed by a wall and defensive ditches. By the time a monastery got this big, however, the monk himself was usually long dead and his bones or other relics formed the holy centre. The second focus, of course, was the rectangular church – first made of wood and later stone. Other holy sites were also often found within the monasteries' walls – sacred wells or stones, for example,

'Let your life be completely detached from the world, and follow the teaching of Christ and the Gospels.'

THE RULE OF
COLUMBA

'A melodius bell, pealing out over the glen, such is the will of the fair Lord, that many brothers may be gathered under one discipline.'

THE RULE OF THE
GRAY MONKS

usually associated with miracles of the monastery's founding saint.

Even the less-holy places were laid out with regard to spiritual importance. Great open courtyards separated the church and other buildings. These mainly consisted of living and working quarters and storage sheds (valuables were later placed in the famous round towers that can still be seen at many monasteries today, but these were not constructed until the 10th century at the earliest). Some monasteries had dormitories, but individual sleeping quarters seem to be more common, housing a monk, two, three, or seven or more. Some of the most magnificent ones remaining can be found on Skellig (meaning 'steep rock of') Michael. The island the monastery sits on, 18 miles off Ireland's southwest coast, is 715 feet high, but only 2,000 feet long. It is not even large enough for the traditional circular enclosure, so the monastery's walls wander all over the rocks. Inside the enclosure was a garden, a graveyard, two chapels, and six rocky 'beehive' cells that still stand. In each of these, one or two monks slept and worked.

Skellig Michael stayed small, its isolation and limited space protecting it from growth. Many other Irish monasteries, however, continued to expand, eventually housing hundreds of clerics and countless more laity. At the turn of the first millennium, the monastery Ard Macha had thousands of residents. (Other monasteries had similar claims – 4,000 at Bangor, 3,000 at Clonmacnoise – but these may be severely inflated.) Ireland had been a fully rural island before Christianity took root. The monasteries became the island's first cities – and only a few of its residents were monks. The rest formed a kind of support structure for the monastery, with metal smiths, farmers, stable keepers, carpenters and others lay workers. Adding to that were the myriad visitors continually entering and exiting. 'Who can count the different crowds and numberless peoples flocking in from all the provinces,' wrote one hagiographer. 'Some for the abundant feasting,

'If you have withdrawn from the world, remember that you now walk a path of suffering. Do not look to the world, but rather flee from it as you would from a hue and cry.'

THE RULE OF
COMGALL

others for the healing of their afflictions, others to watch the pageant of the crowds, others with great gifts and offerings.'

The monastic rules and penitentials

Guiding the monastery's life were rules set down by the founder. For centuries these were probably unwritten, but followed nonetheless. It was not until a group of monastic reformers known as the Céli Dé (Clients of God) instituted a widespread revival in the 700s and 800s that the surviving rules were put to paper. The rule attributed to Comgall (c. 517–602), probably written in the late 700s, begins with an overview 'to love Christ, to shun wealth, to remain close to the heavenly king, and to be gentle towards all people'. It also included such directives as ordering monks to prostrate themselves on the floor 100 times in the morning and again in the evening while chanting psalms. 'If this is done,' the rule says, 'his reward will be great in the kingdom of heaven.' Hundreds more prostrations during the day were also prescribed. Reciting each of the 150 psalms daily was encouraged. During Lent, self-beatings were added. The rule also warns against too much of a good thing: 'Do not practise long, drawn-out devotions, but rather give yourself to prayer at intervals, as you would to food. Pious humbug is an invention of the devil.'

An even more rigorous monastic literature came in the form of penitential books. These apparently rose from a practical theological problem in the church: What do you do with sinning Christians? Believers who had undergone baptism were believed to have been washed free of the guilt of sin – it had all been forgiven. But sins committed after baptism, especially serious sins such as apostasy, murder and fornication could only be undone with penance. For much of the Christian world, though, there was a second problem – you only got one shot at penance. It could not be repeated – second offences meant damnation. So what do you do when someone sins after penance?

'What a wonderful road it is to remain faithful to self-denial, and to be eager for it. Let the monk daily bear in mind that he will die, and let him be zealous in his concern for every person.'

THE RULE OF COMGALL

Skellig Michael's small, hilly enclosure held six huts, two chapels, a graveyard and a garden.

For the Celtic monks, penance was not just a one-time attempt at securing entrance into heaven. All offences, from wanting to hit someone to actually murdering him, were slips along a road to sinless perfection. Sins were symptoms of a disease, not a one-time decision for good or evil. Penance therefore was not a ticket; it was therapy. 'A variety of offences make for a variety of penances,' says the *Penitential of Columbanus*. 'And as physicians have to make a variety of medicines, so spiritual doctors must have different cures for the different wounds, ailments, pains, weaknesses of the soul.'

In most cases, especially in the *Penitential of Columbanus*, the medicine fitted the disease in predictable ways: 'The talkative is to be punished with silence, the restless with the practice of gentleness, the gluttonous with fasting, the sleepy with watching, the proud with imprisonment, the deserter with expulsion.' Other sins were spelled out more exactly – stealing meant a year on bread and water. A celibate monk fathering a child deserved seven years on such meagre sustenance. Fornication without fatherhood brought between three and twelve years of the penance, depending on the height of clerical office.

Other penitentials offer different courses, but still see them as remedies. 'If anyone has sinned in his heart through thought,' says the *Penitential of Finnian*, 'and then at once has repented, let him strike his breast, and ask God for pardon, and make satisfaction, and thus he will become well.'

One common penance was work. 'If you labour well you will be content, and if you endure steadily, you will be holy,' says the rule of Molua. The work, however, was not itself holy. Unlike some later continental monks who saw all labour as sacred, or even as a form of prayer, Celtic Christians saw a split between their devotional life and their secular work – and the sacred always won out. One young monk, Mochuda, was supposed to be tending swine when he heard a retinue of monks chanting psalms. He

immediately abandoned the swine – the livelihood
of his family – to join in. Later he, like many other
monks in the hagiographies, found other ways to neglect
manual labour. Holy magic or angels would power mills
while monks studied and slept. When heaven did not
intervene, manual labour was something best left to the
professionals. A monk's day was best served in holier
service.

What a monk actually did with his day depended on
his relative status. A poem from the 11th century listed
the job descriptions of one monastic community:

*Psalm-singer, beginning student, historian (who is not
insignificant), instructor, teacher of ecclesiastical law, head
teacher with great knowledge, bishop, priest and deacon,
subdeacon (a noble course), lector, porter, swift exorcist…
vice-abbot, cook (proper and right), counsellor, steward,
alternate vice-abbot…*

Undereducated newcomers might simply be farmers
with vows. Those who had grown up at the monastery
were highly educated and typically given the duties more
associated with Celtic monks – singing, studying, praying
and writing.

Prayers of the Celts

Much has been made of Celtic prayers and the way
Celtic monks prayed, but for the most part they prayed
like the rest of Christian Europe at the time. Surviving
manuscripts of prayers used in Mass, baptism and healing
are very similar to those used elsewhere, and they are
almost always in Latin. The apparent favourite prayer
was Psalm 118, known as the *Beati*. 'Give thanks to the
Lord for he is good,' the psalm begins. 'His love endures
forever.'

'As a man at the foot of the gallows would pour
out praise and lamentation to the king, to gain his
deliverance,' one monk wrote, 'so we pour forth

lamentation to the King of Heaven in the *Beati*, to gain our deliverance.'

Indeed, the *Beati* is not just a psalm of praise; it is also a prayer of protection. 'All the nations surrounded me, but in the name of the Lord I cut them off,' it says. 'They surrounded me on every side, but in the name of the Lord I cut them off. They swarmed around me like bees, but they died out as quickly as burning thorns; in the name of the Lord I cut them off.'

This protective repetition is reflected in many of the vernacular Celtic prayers, especially the *Loricae*. Other protective prayers became more like magical incantations, such as a prayer against headache that went 'Head of Christ, eye of Isaiah, forehead of Noah, lips and tongue of Solomon, throat of Timothy, mind of Benjamin, chest of Paul, joint of John, faith of Abraham: Holy, Holy, Holy, Lord God of Hosts.'

Most prayers, however, focused on prayer, not pragmatism:

Lord, be it thine,
  unfaltering praise of mine!
To thee my whole heart's love be given
  of earth and Heaven Thou King Divine!

Perhaps the best known of the ancient Irish prayers is one from the 700s, which begins: 'Rob tu mo bhoile, a Comdi cride, Ni ni nech aile, acht ri sect nime.' The poem was not translated into English until last century, however. Its 1905 version began, 'Be thou my vision, O Lord of my heart. None other is aught but the King of the seven heavens. Be thou my meditation by day and night; May it be thou that I behold even in my sleep.'

The monks practised beholding God even in their sleep. Each night they would arise at midnight, 3 a.m. and 6 a.m. for liturgical prayers. They even wore their long tunics and hooded cloaks to bed so they would not be detained on their way to pray. 'Do not sleep until it is necessary,' says the rule of Columba. Another rule, listing the characteristics of a holy clerical life, adds 'curtailment of sleep' to the list, between 'perseverance in reading' and 'facility in the reading of history'. Apparently the Celtic monks were no less prone than today's scholars to drift off during their studies.

Saintly scholars

They were also scribblers, writing in the margins of the books they copied. Sometimes they complained about their work. Sometimes they criticized each other's work. At other times, they reacted to what they were copying. 'I am greatly grieved at the aforementioned death,' one wrote after copying the killing of Hector at Troy. Still other times, they daydreamed. 'He is a heart,' wrote one. 'An acorn from the oakwood. He is young. Kiss him!' Another wrote even more scandalously, 'All are keen / To know who'll sleep with the blond Aideen. / All Aideen herself will own / Is that she will not sleep alone.'

One Irish monk described his surroundings as he copied a Latin manuscript by Priscian sometime in the 800s:

A hedge of trees surrounds me, a blackbird's lay sings to me,
praise I shall not conceal,
Above my lined book the trilling of the birds sings to me.
A clear-voiced cuckoo sings to me in a grey cloak from the
tops of bushes.
May the Lord save me from Judgment; well do I write
under the greenwood.

About the time that poem was written, another scribe also described his life – and that of his pet.

I and Pangur Bán, my cat,
'tis a like task we are at;
hunting mice is his delight,
hunting words I sit all night.

'The clear-voiced bell / On chill wild night God's hours doth tell / Rather in it I'll put my trust / Than in a woman's wanton lust.'

MONASTIC POEM,
TRANSLATED BY
ROBIN FLOWER

'tis a merry thing to see
at our tasks how glad are we,
when at home we sit and find
entertainment to our mind.

'Gainst the wall he sets his eye
full and fierce and sharp and sly;
'gainst the wall of knowledge I
all my little wisdom try.

So in peace our task we ply,
Pangur Bán, my cat, and I;
in our arts we find our bliss,
I have mine and he has his.

They may have been occasionally distracted, but it is clear that most monks had a love for learning. 'Better far than praise of men it is to sit with book and pen,' one wrote. By copying the major works of both the Christian world and the classical world, and by being the first to write down many of the stories of the pre-Christian Celtic world, the monks made a great contribution to history and to learning in general. However, Thomas Cahill's famous declaration that this was 'how the Irish saved civilization' is more than an overstatement (the Irish certainly were not the only ones with old manuscripts), but the monks' scholarly work remains a tremendous legacy.

There were plenty of contemporary benefits for the monasteries' educational work, too. The communities drew support from the clan *Túaths* that formed the local governments. In exchange for the land, the monastery educated the *Túath* children. According to at least one agreement, one out of each seven boys educated would become a monk. The monastery must have had its reasons for the clause, but in retrospect it seems unnecessary – young Irish men flocked to the monasteries at an amazing rate.

Finding a soul friend

One of the most important parts of monastic community life was the practice of *anamchara* or 'soul friend'. The term literally means 'one who shares my cell', as soul friends were often cell mates. But there is more than friendship in the term; more importantly, it has an element of mentoring and discipleship. The idea was not unique to the Celtic Christians; even Solomon repeatedly stresses the need for spiritual teamwork in Proverbs and Ecclesiastes: 'As iron sharpens iron, so one man sharpens another' (Proverbs 27:17). For Celtic Christians, however,

'Better far than praise of men it is to sit with book and pen,' an Irish monk wrote in the 9th century. Page from an English manuscript.

it was more than just a good idea. When a young monk's anamchara died, the famous abbess Brigid (whom we will meet in a moment) told him, 'Anyone without a soul friend is a body without a head. Eat no more until you find a soul friend.'

The position may have been of prime importance, but it still had its challenges. 'The office of a spiritual father is a difficult one since, when he prescribes a true remedy, more often than not it is ignored,' says the rule of the Céli Dé. 'But on the other hand, if the spiritual father does not give advice, the culpability is his alone... To point out to them where salvation lies is always better, even if they ignore the confessor's advice.'

If a soul friend slackened in his duties, some monastic communities held him responsible for his disciple's sins. Those duties, recounted in the 9th-century rule of Carthage, include 'chanting intercessions at each canonical hour when the bells are rung', '[daily performing] two hundred genuflections while chanting the *Beati* and the recitation of the three fifties (all 150 psalms)', and 'instruct[ing] the unlearned that they may bend to your will'. One of the most important duties tied back into the penitentials: hearing confession. 'If you are a soul friend to a man, do not barter his soul; do not be as the blind leading the blind; do not leave him in neglect,' the rule of Carthage begins its instructions. 'Let penitents confess to you with candour and integrity.' As with penance, confession was medicinal; it did not necessarily clear away the record of sin so the sinner could get into heaven. 'Frequent confession is useless if the transgressions are also frequent,' says the rule of the Céli Dé.

One saint closely associated with the practice of anamchara is Comgall (c. 517–602), an Irish Pict who founded one of the island's most important monasteries at Bangor around 558. When he lost his soul friend, a bishop named Fiacre who worked in Brittany, Comgall echoed the words of Brigid: 'My soul friend has died and

I am headless.' Maintaining mentorship was so important to Comgall that he made it a requirement of his monastery. After clerical training, each monk was required to become a 'father of others' and to lead spiritual families. Ironically, Comgall had initially wanted to be out on his own, a wandering missionary like Patrick. When his bishop told him not to do so, Comgall turned to another path – radical austerity. He took several friends to an island to live a life emulating the harshest of desert monks. For many of Comgall's friends, it was too harsh: seven died of starvation after he ordered them to fast for days on end. This severe lifestyle continued after the founding of Bangor, but that did not stop the Celtic youth from joining him. By the time Comgall died, more than 3,000 monks had him as their spiritual father, among them some of the most renowned Celtic monks in the world.

Not all monks lived so severely. Even among the Céli Dé, who fought against growing laziness in the monasteries, some criticized extensive asceticism. 'A time will come to him before his death when he shall not perform a single genuflection,' one leader grumbled after witnessing a monk's passion for prostration.

Brigid, Ireland's un-ascetic patroness

One of Ireland's most famous saints obviously disagreed with many rules against alcohol. 'I should like to have a great pool of ale for the King of Kings; I should like the heavenly host to be drinking it for all eternity,' prayed Brigid (c. 454–524) according to an 8th-century retelling. 'I should like there to be cheerfulness for their sake; I should like Jesus to be there too.'

According to the legends, Brigid would have had little trouble making a great pool of ale for the King of Kings – in a twist on Jesus' ability to turn water into wine, she was able to turn it into beer. Another legend gives credit to Brigid for *wanting* to be ascetic but claims heaven forbade it. After one night of praying in a freezing pond, she

'Put in its simplest form, [the] general theology of Celtic Christians thinks of the divine being and act, or better, the divine presence and power, flowing in and through what can only be described as an extended family.'

JAMES MACKEY,
CELTIC SPIRITUALITY

returned the next evening to find it dry. The next morning the water was replenished, but each night as she prepared to mortify herself it was empty again.

Brigid's life is full of miracle, myth and legend – perhaps more so than any other Celtic saint. This may be a result of her story becoming enmeshed with that of another Brigid, a Celtic fertility goddess of fire and song. Indeed, many of her stories are that of fertility. She touches a wooden altar and it becomes 'as green as if the sap still flowed from the roots of a flourishing tree'. She touches a cow and it produces an endless stream of milk. She reinvigorates a wife's sexual attraction for her

Brigid and the fox

One day, says Cogitosus's *Life of Brigid*, a man saw a fox walking into the royal palace. A crowd had gathered, but no one did anything to save the king from such a nasty animal, so the man took action and killed it. Unfortunately, 'it was a pet, familiar with the king's hall, which entertained the king and his companions with various tricks that it had learned – both requiring intelligence and nimbleness of body'. The king was furious, and sentenced the man to death, along with his wife and sons.

Then Brigid enters the story. Upon hearing the poor man's plight, she jumped into her chariot to go convince the king to change his mind. Along the way, she prayed that God would help her in her pursuit, and he did. Another fox jumped out from its den on the plain and into Brigid's chariot. At the palace, the king refused to hear her pleas for the man's life, so Brigid introduced the fox. 'It went through all the tricks that the other fox had performed, and amused the crowd in exactly the same way,' Cogitosus says. It worked – the prisoner and his family were set free. But that is not the end of the story. 'The same fox, bothered by the crowds, skilfully contrived a safe escape. It was pursued by large numbers of riders and hounds, but made fools of them, fled through the plains, and went into the waste and wooded places and so to its den.' For some reason, Cogitosus records, these events caused everyone to venerate Brigid.

husband. In another story, she has control over fertility in another way – she prays over a pregnant nun shamed by her predicament and the unborn child miraculously disappears.

The goddess Brigid, daughter of 'the good god' Dagda, was apparently beloved by the pagan Irish. The saint Brigid appears even more popular among Celtic Christians. She is patron to scholars and poets (as well as milkmaids and many other professions), and her name is now on churches around the world – more than even Patrick. She is the patroness of Ireland, 'dove among birds, vine among trees, sun among stars'. She is 'Mary of the Gael'.

Brigid's beginnings are historically unknowable, but there are many wonderful legends. They say she was the daughter of the noble poet Dubhthach and his Christian concubine Brocseach, but was raised by a druid at least until her baptism. Taken back into her father's home, her gifts of charity – in the Robin Hood sense of the term – were first revealed. 'Whatever her hands would find or would get of her father's wealth and food and property she gave to the poor and needy of the Lord,' says her hagiographer. Her infuriated father attempted to sell Brigid into marriage, but the prospective king he tried to sell her to wanted to know why she had given away her father's sword. 'The Virgin Mary's Son knows, if I had your power, with all your wealth, and with all your land, I would give them all to the Lord of the Elements.' The king preferred his status and wealth to Brigid. 'It is not right for us to deal with this young woman, for her merit before God is higher than ours,' he told Dubhthach. Later, even Brigid's monastery would complain that she was giving away too much of their necessities.

With seven other girls Brigid became a nun, but one story has her as the only female bishop in the church. The *Old Life of Brigid* says that Mel of Ardagh, 'through the grace of the Holy Spirit', accidentally read the wrong prayer at her consecration. He had made her a bishop, not a nun. When the error was pointed out, Mel replied, 'I do not have any power in this matter. That dignity has been given by God to Brigid, beyond every other woman.' She certainly seems to have had considerable power for her time, influencing churches around Ireland and joining conferences with abbots and bishops.

Brigid's monastery also apparently had pagan roots. Kildare means 'Church of the Oak'. It may simply have been named for a nearby tree, but oaks were important to the druids and Brigid may have Christianized a pagan site. She would not have been the only one to do so, but she was unique in Ireland in founding Kildare as a double monastery (that is, one for both men and women). A man named Conlaed oversaw the monks while Brigid oversaw

Extreme Íte

Another famous abbess, Íte, was born Deirdre and was described by her hagiographer as 'a second Brigid'. Apart from being important women in the Irish church, the comparison does not hold up. Her thirst (Iota) for asceticism and holiness earned her the name she is known by today, and she sometimes even outpaced the severity of her contemporaries – male and female. A hagiography from the 900s says she always carried a large stag-beetle under her clothes, where it gnawed on her constantly. When it escaped, one of Íte's nuns killed it, much to the abbess's dismay. 'Where has my fosterling gone?' she lamented. 'For that deed, no nun shall ever rule after me.' Another story recounts how Íte fasted for two, three, or even four days at a time. Finally God sent an angel to tell her, 'You are afflicting your body with too much fasting; you should not do so.' When Íte refused to ease her asceticism, the angel replied, 'God has given you this grace: from this day until your death, you will be refreshed by heavenly food. You will not be able to refuse to eat when the angel of the Lord comes to you with a meal.' Still, Íte was 'a tolerant, humorous old woman' when she died in 570 (or 577), say the *Annals of Ulster*.

the nuns. The nuns, in turn, watched over a sacred fire that may have been originally maintained by pre-Christian virgins. It was kept alight until the Protestant Reformation shut down all Irish monasteries.

Brigid may have been the only woman in Ireland to found a double monastery, but there were many women saints in the country. Some even combated the anti-female mindset that infused much of Celtic Christianity (with women come sin). Patrick's *Lorica*, for example, invokes protection 'against spells cast by women, smiths, and druids'. Kevin avoided the sound of sheep, knowing that sheep led to shepherdesses, which led to temptation. Cannera found this same attitude when she went to Sénán's monastery at Scattery Island. The abbot would not let her, nor any other woman enter the enclosure. 'Christ is no worse than you,' she rebuked him. 'He came to redeem women no less than to redeem men. He suffered for the sake of women as much as for the sake of men.

The ruins of Killeevy, founded by the abbess Monenna.

Women as well as men can enter the heavenly kingdom. Why, then should you not allow women to live on this island?'

'You are persistent,' Sénán replied, and relented.

Monenna was the abbess of Cell-Sléibhe-Cuilinn (now known as Killeevy), one of the most prominent women's monasteries of Ireland. She supposedly took her vows from Patrick himself, but one of her more dramatic tales was an encounter with Kevin, the ascetic monk who avoided women by avoiding sheep. Hearing that Monenna had been praying with a thief and raider, Kevin flew into a fury. He was determined to destroy her monastery. Calmly, the abbess exorcised Kevin's jealousy and even drew a hot bath to calm him.

As the story of Kevin and Monenna shows, the Celtic monks were not always the tranquil, peace-loving

Principal early monasteries with their founders and dates

Major Celtic royal centres

ATLANTIC OCEAN

Derry
(Columba, 546)

Lough Neagh

Bangor
(Comgall, c. 558)

Emain Macha

Armagh
(attributed to Patrick, 444)

Cruachu

Kells
(attributed to Columba)

Lough Ree

Clonmacnoise
(Ciaran, 548)

Tara

Clonard
(Finnian, 520)

Kildare
(Brigid, c. 468)

Lough Corrib

Clonfert
(Brendan, 561)

Inishmore
(Énda, 484)

Galway Bay

Glendalough
(Kevin, 6th century)

Durrow
(Columba, c. 556)

IRISH SEA

Cashel

Skellig Michael
(c. 588)

Bantry Bay

CELTIC SEA

clergy some books make them seem. Rivalries between monasteries for power, glory and wealth were common. In fact, this is the main reason there are so many hagiographies. The monasteries were eager to showcase the power of their founding saint. In some cases, the hagiographies contain extensive travels and monasteries founded by the saint, arguing that the successor of whatever saint got there first still commanded authority in that region. In other cases, stories were told to literally assert a monastery was 'holier than thou'. Miracle stories would be told to suggest not-so-subtly that 'my saint can beat up your saint'.

It was not just a matter of bragging rights. Powerful monasteries held more political sway with local kings and even commanded tribute and rent from less powerful ones. The *Tripartite Life of Patrick* claimed that every church member in the town of Airtech owed Patrick's 'chief seat' of Armagh one calf each. 'And that this tribute is not given to them causes the community of Patrick to sigh,' the hagiography adds.

Tírechán also wrote his Patrick hagiography and other works to promote Armagh's superiority over other monasteries. In one passage, Patrick tells a monastery's founder, 'Thy seed will be blessed, and from thy seed will come priests of the Lord and worthy leaders owing alms to me and remaining your heirs.' Apparently that monastery was not paying, either. Tírechán described Óno and his family as 'the kindred of dogshit'.

Attacks were not just verbal. In 836, the monks of Armagh attacked the double monastery at Kildare; the followers of Patrick and of Brigid went to battle.

Such behaviour certainly was not condoned by the founding saints. 'If any cleric has committed murder and killed his neighbour, let him do penance for ten years in exile; after these, let him be restored to his native land, if he has performed his penance well on bread and water,' says the *Penitential of Columbanus*. 'But if he does not make satisfaction to [the slain's] relatives, let him never

The principal early monasteries of Ireland, with the names and dates of their founders.

be restored to his native land, but like Cain let him be a wanderer and a fugitive upon the earth.'

Sometimes such wanderings were prescribed for penitence. In other cases (including that of the credited penitential writer himself), leaving one's homeland was done voluntarily.

Columba and Scotland

'Columba never could spend the space of even one hour without study, or prayer, or writing, or some other holy occupation,' wrote the saint's hagiographer, Adomnán. According to tradition, he loved his studies too much. Studying under Finnian of Moville, Columba came across a beautiful manuscript of the psalms and Gospels, and simply had to have it. So he copied it – without Finnian's permission. When the abbot discovered the duplicate, he was infuriated and demanded that Columba surrender it. The monk refused. Finnian then appealed to Díarmait mac Cerbaill, the high king of Tara and a relative of Columba. But the monk's family ties did him no good. 'To every cow her calf,' the king ruled, 'and to every book its copy.'

About that same time, Díarmait reportedly offended Columba in another way, ordering the execution of one of the monk's young followers – and a prince to boot. Doubly angered, Columba rallied his tribe, the northern Uí Néill, and in the battle of Cúl Dreimne slaughtered 3,000 of Díarmait's men. Recent historians attribute the battle to a dispute over who would

The Cathach, or 'Battle Book', from around AD 560–630, is the oldest surviving Irish manuscript for the Psalter Columba is said to have copied illicitly.

The Mound of the
Hostages at the
Hill of Tara in
County Meath,
Ireland. Tara
remained a seat
of political power
after Christianity
became dominant
on the island.

succeed Díarmait as king of Tara and say Columba had
nothing to do with it. Still, for centuries the 'Cathach' book
of Columba would be one of the Celtic world's most famous
(and allegedly powerful) relics. More than half of the
manuscript is missing, and when in 1813 it was removed
from its wooden box, which was enclosed in a silver case,
its 58 nine-by-six-inch leaves were stuck together. Still,
careful analysis of the psalter suggests that it might
actually be from the hand of Columba. Its name, meaning
'battler', comes not from the battle of Cúl Dreimne but
from later medieval battles where chiefs paraded it around
their army three times to ensure victory.

For Columba, tradition says, victory was short.
His soul friend, Molaise of Devenish, assigned him
the common penance for causing such carnage – exile.
Specifically, Molaise prescribed, Columba should leave
Ireland to convert as many souls as had been slain at Cúl
Dreimne. A large task indeed, but Columba's legacy would
be even bigger.

Royal fox, holy dove

Columba was born for greatness – but all signs indicated
that it would be political, not spiritual. He was born on
5 December 521 to Fedilmidh, the great-grandson of one
of the most famous Irish political heroes (and one of
the earliest undisputed Irish historical figures), Niall

Noígiallch, or Niall of the Nine Hostages. His namesake
clan, the Uí Néill, invaded Ulster and created a dynasty.
Columba may even have been a contender for the throne
at Tara. His mother, Ethne, was also reportedly from a
powerful family, descending from Leinster king Cathoair
Mór. That Columba grew up in the monasteries was simply
a matter of course. As noted earlier, many monasteries
were given land in exchange for the education of the royal
youth. Like Columba, many of these young men never left
the life of the church. Columba was reportedly even more
eager than many of these, however. His childhood friends
waited for him to finish his psalm-reading so often that
it was they who nicknamed him 'Colum Cille', meaning
'dove of the church'. (There is some dispute over whether
his given name was Colum, meaning 'dove', or Crimthann,
meaning 'fox'. In any case, hagiographers and biographers
alike have enjoyed using these zoological appellations as
a way of characterizing him – crafty and peaceful, sly and
holy.)

Growing up, Columba followed several different
monastic leaders, including a priest named Cruithnecin,
Finnian of Moville (who had studied at Candida Casa), and
Finnian of Clonard. He also studied under a Christian bard
named Gemmán, whose vocation Columba would later
defend to the Irish church. When the monk reached his mid-
thirties, Finnian of Clonard pushed to make him a bishop,

*'The personality
of Columcille,
which gleams
through all his
works and all
the tales we
know of him,
convinces us
that he is
Patrick's
spiritual son
and worthy
successor.'*

THOMAS CAHILL,
*HOW THE IRISH
SAVED CIVILIZATION*

A page from the
Book of Durrow,
created in the
second half of
the 7th century.

*'He was
learning's
pillar in every
stronghold, he
was foremost at
the book of
complex Law.
The northern
land shone, the
western people
blazed, he lit
up the east with
chaste clerics.'*

MEMORIAL AFTER
COLUMBA'S DEATH

but Columba's story became the opposite of that of bishopess Brigid. In another ordination mistake, Columba was consecrated as a mere priest. Like the mistake at Brigid's consecration, the error was seen as divine providence. Columba said he would never accept higher rank.

After returning for a time to Clonard, Columba joined Comgall (later of Bangor) in helping another monk, Mobhi, start a monastery at Glasnevin. Unfortunately, an outbreak of the plague crushed the monks' plans and the site was abandoned. Columba then founded his own monastery, at Derry. After that he founded more. One hagiography says he founded a total of 300 before his death. An 1857 study counted more than 40 in Ireland and another 57 in Scotland. But only two sites meet today's strict tests for attribution – Durrow and Kells. The latter is the site of that great illustrated manuscript of the Gospels, the *Book of Kells*, said to be the work 'not of men, but of angels'. Adomnán says Columba himself was similarly angelic:

Devoted from childhood to the Christian novitiate and the study of philosophy, preserving by God's favour integrity of body and purity of soul, he showed himself, though placed on earth, ready for life in heaven; for he was angelic in aspect, refined in speech, holy in work, excellent in ability, great in council.

The founding of Iona

No doubt Columba might have been one of the greatest monastic leaders Ireland has ever known – but it is Scotland he is most associated with. Admonán leaves out the story of the Cathach copyright tiff and any suggestion that Columba's sojourn across the Irish Sea might be a form of penance. But he does mention the battle. 'In the second year following the battle of Cúl Dreimne, when he was 41, Columba sailed away to Britain, choosing to be a pilgrim for Christ.'

'Delightful I think it to be in the bosom of an isle on the crest of a rock, that I may see often the calm of the sea,' Columba wrote. 'That I may see its heavy waves over the glittering ocean as they chant a melody to their Father on their eternal course.' He found that island half a mile west of yet another island, the Island of Mull in the Inner Hebridean islands off Scotland's west coast.

Iona (also called Í, or Hii) is only three miles long by a mile and a half wide. Of its 2,000 acres, only 500 are arable. But even before Columba arrived, it had apparently been considered sacred Christian ground. The kings of the Gaelic Dál Riada kingdom were buried here in ground either consecrated by or dedicated to St Oran (d. 549). Columba's hagiography even includes a story of the saint encountering two bishops shortly after landing on the island. 'But God revealed to Columba that they really were not bishops,' the story says. 'They left the island when he told them of their duplicity.' Today Iona is still considered sacred ground, one of the top pilgrimage sites in all Britain. It is not easy to get to, and seems nearly as remote as holy Skellig Michael off the coast of Ireland. Still, when Columba and his 12 disciples landed on Iona's pebbled beach on 12 May 563, they probably did not see it as the isolated centre of 'white martyrdom'. Instead, it was a centre of trade and travel. Sea lanes brought goods from France, the Mediterranean and beyond. The island stood at the northern end of the Dál Riada kingdom, ruled by Columba's cousin, Conall mac Comgaill. It was therefore almost a perfect place for launching an evangelistic mission to convert the Picts, whose territory lay beyond Conall's. (The island may actually have been disputed territory between the Dál Riada and the Picts; the English historian Bede claims it was the Pictish king Brude, not Conall, who gave the island to Columba.) Ireland, only 80 miles away, could provide steady support – and monks – for the monastery. In fact, the Dál Riada had only moved its capital to Scotland from Ireland a generation before Columba's arrival.

Nearby islands would be brought under Iona's watch, serving special monastic purposes. On Tiree, laity served penance. Another island housed old monks living out their lives as green martyrs and anchorites. Iona became the centre for educating and training priests, bishops and scholars. Columba's hut was slightly larger than those of his disciples (which included his uncle Ernan and the son of a king) and placed on top of a slight hill. Iona may have been a hub of activity, but Columba's quarters were still austere. 'For straw mattress', Adomnán wrote, Columba used 'a bare rock, and for pillow a stone'. Historian John T. McNeill counts the other buildings that soon followed: 'a refectory with a kitchen; a scriptorium with a library; a guesthouse for the use of the surprisingly numerous visitors from near and far; a smithy, a kiln, a mill, and two barns; and a small church, later enlarged and strengthened with oak beams brought by sea'.

Soon even these buildings were pushed to their limits as recruits came from Scotland, Ireland and Britain. Even Saxons, whose kin were invading Britain from the south, sought peaceful entry into the monastic life at Iona. But the monks of Iona were not just recluses; they were also missionaries. Both the Scots of the Dál Riada and the northern Picts were Columba's evangelistic mission. Exactly how much of the country Columba worked in is some matter of scholarly disagreement, and the historical record is unclear. Unlike many hagiographers, Adomnán did not write his stories to establish his patron's dominion over numerous territories. By his time, Iona was already powerful enough that he did not have to. Instead, Adomnán's task was to keep things that way. Thus he avoided some topics that would have divided his readership, such as Columba's role in the Easter debate (which we shall encounter later). Adomnán's objectives also mean that we do not have long accounts of Columba's travels, though there are a few of these, noting monastic foundations were laid on the islands of Hinba, Tiree and Skye. One of the most important of the saint's trips was to the Pictish king Brude in 564. Adomnán

'*His monks, the laity, even the animals felt his attraction. He could terrify, he could comfort, he could delight.*'

KATHLEEN HUGHES,
*THE CHURCH IN
EARLY IRISH SOCIETY*

Previous pages:
**The rebuilt
remains of a
Benedictine abbey
on the island of
Iona keep watch
over Columba's
island, which is
only 3 miles wide
by 1.5 miles long.**

*'By virtue of his
prayer, and in
the name of our
Lord Jesus
Christ, he healed
several persons
suffering under
various
diseases; and...
expelled from
this our island...
innumerable
hosts of
malignant
spirits, whom
he saw with his
bodily eyes
assailing
himself, and
beginning to
bring deadly
distempers on
his monastic
brotherhood.'*

ADOMNÁN,
LIFE OF COLUMBA

provides no narrative of this meeting, only a series of
miracle stories. They begin at the very entrance to Brude's
Inverness fortress, where the king, 'elated by the pride
of royalty, acted haughtily' and closed the gates. Columba
simply made the sign of the cross, then knocked and laid
his hand on the gate. It 'instantly flew open of its own
accord, the bolts having been driven back with great force',
Adomnán says, and Brude and his men forever 'held this
holy and reverend man in very great honour, as was due'.
They may have continued to give him honour, but according
to Adomnán, Columba kept working miracles in front
of the king, such as floating a white stone 'like an apple
when placed in water'. When some druids tried to stop the
monks from singing praises to God, Columba began singing
Psalm 44. 'So wonderfully loud, like pealing thunder, did his
voice become, that king and people were struck with terror
and amazement,' the hagiographer wrote. Unfortunately,
Adomnán left no stories about any conversations between
the chief and the monk, though Bede suggests the king
converted to Christianity.

The Loch Ness monster
On this same journey, Columba's sign of the cross became
handy in another dangerous encounter – the first recorded
sighting of a Loch Ness monster. Columba and his men
were attempting to cross the Ness when they encountered
a burial party. A local man had been swimming in the
waters, the mourners explained, when the monster had
savaged him. It was no matter to Columba. He turned
to one of his monks, Lugne Mocumin, and told him to
swim across the river to fetch a boat from the opposite
bank. Lugne disrobed down to his tunic in an instant and
jumped in obediently. 'But the monster, which, so far from
being satiated, was only roused for more prey, was lying
at the bottom of the stream,' Adomnán wrote. 'When it
felt the water disturbed above by the man swimming,
it suddenly rushed out, and, giving an awful roar, darted
after him, with its mouth wide open, as the man swam in

the middle of the stream.' The monks and the burial party were terrified, but not Columba. He simply made the sign of the cross again and told the monster, 'Thou shalt go no further, nor touch the man; go back with all speed.' The monster obeyed, fleeing 'more quickly than if it had been pulled back with ropes'. Adomnán then adds the requisite coda about the pagans in the burial party converting to Christianity after witnessing such a miracle.

Modern Nessie fanatics are divided on the story, suggesting that it was not the 'real' Loch Ness monster after all – it is far too violent, and was seen in the wrong part of the lake. But an Italian geologist offers a different opinion, suggesting that something like the incident may have occurred after all, but that the monks only saw waves caused by an earthquake. 'The most seismically active end of the loch is the north end' where Columba had his encounter, Luigi Piccardi told *The Irish Times*. 'In these reports people don't usually describe the beast itself. More often they talk of seeing a lot of commotion in the water, and hearing loud noises, and they assume it to be caused by the monster.'

Integration of church and state

Columba converted the Picts 'to the Faith of Christ by his preaching and example', Bede records. But he maintained his work among the Dál Riada as well. Here, too, the princely monk ministered among kings. When Conall mac Comgaill died in 574, Columba was on a spiritual retreat on the island of Hinba. Adomnán records that an angel came to him, carrying 'a book of glass, regarding the appointment of kings'. The monk, however, was unwilling to read much of it – he preferred that Gabran ascend to the throne rather than Gabran's brother Aidan, as written in the book. After a beating by the angel, the monk relented and consecrated Aidan at Iona in one of the earliest such ceremonies in British history.

One year after Aidan took the Dál Riada throne, Columba came to his political support again. This time, however, he had to return to Ireland to do it. The trip, which reportedly came near the end of Columba's life, probably was not his only trip back to his homeland, but it was apparently the most important. (A later hagiography, attempting to reconcile Columba's exile and return, records that he always wore a hooded cloak so that he could not see the Irish sky, and always stood on a strip of imported sod from Iona.) One of the main agenda points at the Convention of Druim Cett, or 'conference of kings', was whether the Dál Riada should have to pay tribute to the king of Tara or even become more subservient to the Irish kingdoms. Columba apparently argued persuasively for the independence of Aidan and the kingdom both in Ireland and Scotland. A second agenda item proposed getting rid of the ancient bards. Between their mockery of the powerful, their high fees, and the Christianizing of Ireland, the kings believed it was time to be done with the profession. The saint, who once called Jesus his 'holy druid', saw little harm in the poets' works. On the contrary, he argued, the bards were an important part of Irish society. Yes, sometimes they went too far – and for that they should face discipline and should be forced to be educated at the monasteries – but abolishing their vocation was too harsh an answer. When the kings took the saint's advice, 1,200 bards reportedly burst into the council to sing Columba's praises. Embarrassed, he hid himself inside his cowl.

At the age of 77, back in Iona, an angel again came to Columba and told him he was soon to die. The saint began preparing, making sure that there was enough grain stored for the coming year. On his way to return to the monastery, he came across the packhorse that used to carry the monks' milk pails. Instinctively knowing that his master was about to die, the horse laid its head on Columba's breast. Adomnán writes that the horse 'began to neigh plaintively, and, like a human being, to shed copious tears on the saint's chest'. Columba's assistant, Diarmuid, tried to shoo the horse away, but Columba rebuked him and blessed the horse.

'Scion of the most powerful family in the north of Ireland, founder of monasteries, and instigator of missions to the Picts and the English, Columba is undoubtedly the most important saint associated with Celtic churches.'

THOMAS OWEN
CLANCY,
'IONA'S TOUGH
DOVE', *CHRISTIAN
HISTORY*

Returning to his cell that Saturday, 8 June 597, Columba turned one final time to his lifelong task of copying texts. He ended his psalter at Psalm 34, verse 10: 'The lions may grow weak and hungry, but those who seek the Lord lack no good thing.' 'At the end of the page I must stop. Let Baithene write what follows,' he said. He attended the evening service, then returned to his flagstone bed. There he gave his final instructions to Diarmuid and the other monks:

Be at peace, and have genuine charity among yourselves. If you thus follow the example of the holy fathers, God, the comforter of the good, will be your helper and I, abiding with him, will intercede for you. He will not only give you sufficient to supply the wants of this present life, but will also bestow on you the good and eternal rewards which are laid up for those that keep his commandments.

When the bell rang for the midnight hours, Columba raced from his bed ahead of the monks and prostrated himself in front of the altar. As the monks came in with their lights, Columba raised his hand and blessed them with his final breath.

'There is a grey eye / That will look back upon Erin [Ireland]; / Never again will it see / The men of Erin or women.'

ATTRIBUTED TO
COLUMBA

Iona after Columba

For more than a century, Iona remained one of the most influential sites in Celtic Christianity. Monasteries and churches from Britain and Ireland both looked to the small island for leadership, and Columba was as highly honoured as Patrick and Brigid. When controversies rose, the leaders of Iona were key in the consultations. The island also continued to send out missionaries, into Northumbria, Wessex, and even the continent. Still, the historical record remains sketchy about how much the conversion of Scotland (called Alba by the Celts and Caledonia by the Romans) can be attributed to Iona and how much belongs to other monastic settlements, including Candida Casa. Most likely missionaries came from both the west and the south – and they sometimes even worked together.

One of the best-known evangelists who left from
Iona was an Irish monk named Aidan. But he began as
a substitute. King Oswald of Northumbria had originally
sent a request to the holy island for a teacher, and
Corman, 'another man of more austere disposition'
was the first volunteer. Bede says he was a failure:

*Meeting with no success in his preaching to the English,
who refused to listen to him, he returned home and reported
to his superiors that he had been unable to teach anything
to the nation to whom they had sent him because they
were an uncivilized people of an obstinate and barbarous
temperament.*

As his superiors tried to decide the next step, Aidan
challenged his fellow monk. 'It seems to me that you
were too severe on your ignorant hearers,' he said. 'You
should have followed the practice of the apostles, and
begun by giving them the milk of simpler teaching, and
gradually instructed them in the word of God until they
were capable of greater perfection and able to follow the
sublime precepts of Christ.' The elders then suggested
that Aidan try where Corman had failed. He did, and the
English welcomed him with open arms. Rather than take
up residence in the capital city of Bamburgh, Aidan made
his base on another island, Lindisfarne. It became another
spiritual metropolis of learning and artistry. One of its
most famous creations, the illuminated Lindisfarne
Gospels, are now in the British Library as one of the
world's great artistic treasures. Aidan, meanwhile,
became known by Bede and others as 'the true
apostle of England'.

According to Adomnán, Columba foresaw all
of the glories of Iona and its monks. 'This place,
however small and mean, will have bestowed upon it
no small but great honour by the kings and peoples of
Ireland, and also by the rulers of even barbarous and
foreign nations with their subject tribes,' he said

Facing page:
The first page of
the Gospel of
Matthew in the
Lindisfarne
Gospels, created
around AD 698.

Lindisfarne's
monument to its
founder, Aidan.

near the end of his life. 'And the saints of other churches too will give it great reverence.'

But Adomnán had his own reasons for pushing Iona's continued glory – he himself was Columba's eighth successor as abbot of Iona. Though he is most famous as Columba's hagiographer, Adomnán (624–704) was a significant leader in his own right. He actually shared more of Columba's characteristics than simply his ecclesiastical position – he was actually an Irish blood relative of the earlier saint. And like Columba, Adomnán was a diplomat, engaged in political and ecclesiastic controversies of his day. Like Columba (and Patrick before him) he too worked hard to free hostages. He was a poet, too. But in his scholarship he may have even surpassed his predecessor.

Adomnán also wrote some very important laws. These include regulations on marriage (a man cannot remarry if his wife becomes a prostitute) and theft (Christians cannot accept stolen cattle as gifts or trade), and several outline dietary and health regulations. 'Sea animals found dead on the shore, and where we do not know how they died, can be eaten in good faith; but may not be eaten if they are putrid,' commands one. Another orders, 'A well in which a carcass (whether human, dog, or other animal) is found is to be emptied, all the mud is to be taken out, and then the well will be found clean.' Several of these rules seem like common sense to modern readers, or may remind historians of Old Testament regulations. But people in Adomnán's day knew little about the spread of disease and germs. These rules kept them safe and alive.

The most famous of Adomnán's edicts was 'The Law of the Innocents'. 'These are the four laws of Ireland,' a document from around the 800s says, 'Patrick's law, not to kill the clergy; and Adomnán's law, not to kill women;

Dáire's law, not to kill cattle; and the law of Sunday, not to transgress thereon.' But Adomnán's law was much more than just a prohibition on the killing of women. Enacted in 697 at the Synod of Birr, the law begins with a lengthy introduction about the plight of women and why such a law was needed. Then it describes how an angel came to Adomnán one Pentecost eve and hit him in the side with a staff. 'Go forth into Ireland, and make a law in it that women be not in any manner killed by men, through slaughter or any other death, either by poison, or in water, or in fire, or by any beast, or in a pit, or by dogs, but that they shall die in their lawful bed,' the angel said. The law metes out strict retributions for the slaying of women, including the amputation of the left foot and right hand

The Holy Places

Adomnán did not just copy important theological books; he wrote them. One of them, *The Holy Places* (*De Locis Sanctis*) was one of the most important books of his day, and circulated even more than his *Life of Columba*, which was written more for the community at Iona and those interested in it. He supposedly wrote the book after meeting a Gallic bishop named Arculf, who had been shipwrecked on his way back from a pilgrimage to Jerusalem and made his way to Iona. Historian Thomas O'Loughlin argues, however, that the Arculf story only provides a backbone for Adomnán's extensive research into the geography of the Holy Land, which drew from early church writings and other sources. 'The text shows Adomnán as a most competent and searching scriptural scholar, keenly attuned to textual problems and ingenious in his solutions,' O'Loughlin writes. Bede thought so too, calling the abbot 'a wise man, admirably learned in the scriptures'. The English historian even condensed the work for his own *Holy Places* book.

Like Patrick, Adomnán approached his work with a heavy dose of holy humility. 'I have written down these things in what I admit is a poor style,' he writes at the end of *The Holy Places*. 'But I have done so in the face of daily labour coming at me from all sides. The amount of ecclesiastical concerns seems overwhelming. So I wish that you who read these places not neglect to pray for me, the sinner who wrote this, to Christ the judge of the ages.'

of the killer and the payment of 21 cows from his family (*Cáin Adomnáin* is literally translated 'tax of Adomnán'). The law also protects other non-combatants, such as children and clerics, and includes non-fatal injuries as well: 'If it is a blow with the palm of the hand or with the fist, an ounce of silver [is the fine] for it. If there be a green or red mark, or a swelling, an ounce and six scruples for it.' Rape is of course included in the Law, but also 'seizing women by the hair'. It also guarantees that no 'eye for an eye' justice prevails. 'There shall be no cross-case or balancing of guilt in Adomnán's Law,' it says. 'But each one pays for his crimes for his own hand.'

Adomnán's 'Law of the Innocents' is a landmark in legal history and in the history of human rights. It also demonstrates that by his time, monks were far more than reclusive green martyrs. They often removed themselves for periods of holy solitude, but they were not permanently removed from society. On the contrary, they *were* society. Other monks, however, still desired 'to leave all for the sake of Christ'. These white martyrs, however, would also often find themselves back in public – and thus taking the holy attitudes of their homeland around the known world.

An original copy of Adomnán's *Life of Columba* describes the saint's encounter with a monster from Loch Ness.

Out of, and Back into, the World

'Go from your country and your kindred and your father's house to the land that I will show you,' God told Abraham (Genesis 12:1). For many Celtic Christians, it was more than just a historical urging for the father of the Jews; it was a divine command still to be followed. They left their countries and kindred to enter unknown worlds. Some left in search of greater isolation than could be found on their own island. Others left on evangelistic missions, hoping to bring the light of the gospel to people who had not heard it – or who had forgotten it. Still others, like Brendan of Clonfert, followed Abraham's lead and went looking for a literal 'Promised Land'.

Brendan had heard stories of 'the Promised Land of the Saints, where neither night falls nor day ends'. One visitor to his monastery, a grandson of King Niall named Barinthus, had reportedly even been there. 'We saw only flowering plants and trees that bore fruit,' the visitor had recalled, 'and even the stones were precious.'

Brendan wanted to see the island for himself, but would not without God's blessing. Soon enough it came. 'Arise, O Brendan,' an angel told him. 'For God has given you what you sought, the Land of Promise.' Brendan went to a nearby mountain for fasting and spiritual preparation, and the angel appeared again. 'I will... teach you how to find the beautiful island of which you have had a vision,

A 13th-century manuscript shows and tells the story of Brendan's Easter encounter with the sea creature Jasconius. Such fantastic stories made the *Voyage of Brendan* one of the most popular medieval books.

and which you desire to attain,' he said. Then, says the 10th-century (or so) *Voyage of Brendan*, the saint

… and those with him got iron tools and constructed a light boat ribbed with wood and with a wooden frame, as is usual in those parts. They covered it with ox-hides tanned with the bark of oak and smeared all the joints of the hides on the outside with fat… The also placed a mast in the middle of the boat and a sail and the other requirements for steering a boat.

But after 15 days, the wind died and Brendan and his men rowed to exhaustion. Brendan told his men to rest. 'God is our helper,' he explained. 'He is our navigator and helmsman, and he shall guide us. Pull in the oars and the rudder. Spread the sail and let God do as he wishes with his servants and their boat.' It worked. Every now and then a mysterious wind would blow and change their heading. Likewise, when food ran short, the wind regularly took them to an island. There were several of these, including the Island of Sheep (where the animals grew larger than cows), the Paradise of Birds, and one island that was not quite an island. 'The island was rocky and bare,' the *Voyage* says. 'There were only occasional trees to be seen, and there was no sand on the shoreline at all.' While the rest of the crew went ashore to prepare for Easter Sunday, a discerning Brendan stayed in the boat. After the Easter Mass, the monks had only started to build a cooking fire when 'the island started to heave like a wave'. The monks ran back into the boat and they quickly put two miles between themselves and the island. As they turned to look at the still-burning fire – and many of their

Hell unbound

The sea creature Jasconius was not even the most surprising encounter for Brendan and his crew. One Sunday, the sailors also came upon 'a man, shaggy and unsightly, sitting on a rock'. The waves pounded him mercilessly, but this did not upset the man. For him, it was a beautiful but temporary respite from the fires of hell. 'I am unhappy Judas, the most evil traitor ever,' he explained. 'I am not here in accordance with my deserts but because of the ineffable mercy of Jesus Christ.' Brendan even worked to slightly prolong Judas's relief, keeping at bay the demons who had come to drag the betrayer back to hell. Other characters encountered include a disciple of Patrick, who received a visit from the apostle of Ireland – the day after his death – explaining where to bury his body. Even black-faced leprechauns menaced the crew.

items left ashore – Brendan explained what he had
seen earlier in a vision: 'The island that we were on was
nothing other than a sea animal, the foremost of all that
swim in the oceans… Jasconius is its name.' And for the
next several years, Jasconius allowed the monks to return
to its back to celebrate Easter.

After five years on the sea without sighting the Land
of Promise, Brendan and his men returned to Ireland. A
40-day fast later, they were off again. After another 40 days
of sailing, the men finally landed where all the trees bore
fruit and night never fell. A young man ran up and greeted
them. 'This is the land which you have sought for so long,'
he told them. 'You were not able to find it immediately
because God wished to show you his many wonders in the
great ocean. Return now to the land of your birth, taking
with you fruit from this land and as many gems as your
boat can carry… After the passage of many years, this
land will be revealed to your successors when Christians
will be suffering persecution.' They did as they were told,
returning to the Irish monastery.

The rest of Brendan's life story largely consists of the
founding of Irish monasteries. One of them, at Clonfert,
survived until the Protestant Reformation. There are still
more fantastic tales in his hagiography, like his driving
a plague of fleas from a town (not quite as fantastic as
driving the snakes from Ireland, but miraculous enough to
his hagiographer). His life story also includes encounters
with almost all of the great Celtic saints. He was a close
friend of Comgall of Bangor, with whom he visited Columba
at Iona. Íte supposedly advised him on boat-building
between his first and second Atlantic voyages. He sought
out Brigid after hearing a sea monster invoke her name
in a battle with another monster. On a visit to Wales, he
stayed with Gildas. He was even reportedly baptized by
Erc, one of Patrick's earliest converts. Then there are his
encounters with the lesser known saints, including Énda
and the 'Twelve Apostles of Ireland' (of which he was one).

Such associations may have done more to enhance the

reputations of the other saints than Brendan's. The *Voyage of Brendan* was one of the most popular books of the Middle Ages, translated from Latin into half a dozen or more languages. Whether it was read then as a complex theological allegory, questionable hagiography, or a realistic account of historical events is unknown, but by the end of the 20th century debate was fierce over the story's credibility. Some scholars in the 1960s argued that the islands of sheep and birds were in fact the Faroes; that the Island of Smiths (where 'the sea began to boil as if a volcano were erupting there, with smoke rising from the sea as if from a flaming surface') was volcanic Iceland; that the clear-watered region of fish and whales was near Greenland, and associated other

A model of an
Irish *currach*,
which is usually
made of wood
and leather.

areas with North America. (The arguments themselves were old enough – in 1580, influential mathematician and occultist John Dee made Brendan's voyage a key part of his claim that Britain laid claim to the New World.) The Island of Grapes, one scholar asserted, could have been Jamaica; another postulated that Brendan's episode of the ocean calming 'like a thick curdled mass' must have taken place at the seaweed-heavy Sargasso Sea east of the Bahamas (there are those who say the ancient Phoenicians made it to the Sargasso Sea as well). In 1976, after incredulous historians had reminded Brendan enthusiasts that the story was allegorical – not to mention impossible – British explorer Tim Severin created his own boat just as Brendan's was described. Sailing past the Faroes, Iceland and Greenland – and even encountering friendly whales along the way – Severin's boat was punctured by floating ice. After repairs, he continued on to Newfoundland, suggesting that Brendan *could* have made it to North America in the mid-500s even if he did not. (Of course, returning to Ireland against wind and currents would have been another matter.)

Squeezed out
Whether or not travelling Irish monks made it to America, it is certain they made it at least as far as Iceland in their

Is this Ogham script (and what appears to be a Christian *Chi-Rho* symbol) evidence of early Irish settlement in West Virginia?

white martyrdom searches for isolated monasteries. The Norse *Islendingabok* by Ari the Learned says that when the first Norwegian explorers arrived on the island in 874, they found that the monks had been there for about 80 years:

The Christians, whom the Norsemen called Papar, were here. But afterwards they went away because they did not wish to

The first Irish-Americans?

Stone carvings in West Virginia appear to be Old Irish writings using the old Ogham alphabet. Christian symbols, such as the chi-rho, are also inscribed. 'It seems possible that the scribes that cut the West Virginia inscriptions may have been Irish missionaries in the wake of Brendan's voyage, for these inscriptions are Christian,' argued the late linguist Barry Fell. 'Early Christian symbols of piety… appear at the sites together with the Ogham texts.' Other historians and archaeologists are not as credulous, although at least one respected archaeologist, the University of Calgary's David Kelley, defended Fell's findings. 'I have no personal doubts that some of the inscriptions which have been reported are genuine Celtic Ogham,' he wrote in *Review of Archaeology*.

Every six years,
pilgrims recreate
Ronán's journey
at *La grande
Troménie* in
Locronan,
Brittany.

live here together with heathen men, and they left behind Irish books, bells, and crooks. From this it could be seen that they were Irish.

Several centuries earlier, the ethnic relatives of those Irish monks had been forced out of their homes by the distant relatives of the Norsemen – Angles and Saxons from Denmark. By the middle of the 400s, homeless British refugees were swarming Brittany, originally called Armorica by both Celts and Romans (from the Celtic words *ar*, 'on', and *môr*, 'the sea'). Soon there were so many Britons living there they began to call it Britannia Minor (or, by those who lived there, simply Britannia). The land was sparsely populated enough that there are no accounts of violence between the Britons and the area's original inhabitants, but there are also no reliable stories of how Christianity first came to the area. We think we know, however, how Celtic Christianity grew in the area. As it was back in Britain and Ireland, monks probably came to the area seeking holy seclusion, but they attracted disciples and laity who needed the services a monastery could provide. Clergy probably led some groups of immigrants from Britain, and other monks probably left their homeland expressly to minister to the displaced throngs. We have already met, for example, Illtud and Samson of Dol, both associated with Brittany monasteries.

One of the earliest remembered monks is an Irishman named Ronán. The son of two of Patrick's converts, he went south around the year 500 and is still actively remembered today, especially at Locronan's *La grande Troménie*, a pilgrim processional remembering one of the saint's most memorable stories. A farmer near Ronán's hermitage lost a sheep to a hungry wolf, who returned it unharmed at the monk's demand. The awed farmer converted to Christianity, but his wife, Keben, sensed evil. Ronán was able to command the wolf, she argued, because he was a werewolf! She set about to prove her point, but was repeatedly rebuffed. When she hid her child in a chest

'A spirit of restless energy possessed them. It was given many names, but its cause must surely be sought in the peculiarly Irish development of Christianity in the early centuries: a seeking curiosity, the desire to expand mental boundaries along with physical, to find new ideas in new settings.'

KATHERINE
SCHERMAN,
*THE FLOWERING
OF IRELAND*

and accused Ronán of eating it, the child died. The saint brought it back to life. Not too long afterwards, Ronán himself died – but his battle with Keben was not over. As four white oxen, carried his body to hermitage without a driver, Keben attacked them, even breaking off one of their horns. God apparently decided Ronán had suffered enough at the woman's hands; the ground opened and swallowed her up. Today's pilgrims now pass the site of the earthquake, 'Keben's Cross', as *La grande Troménie* recreates the oxen's wandering path.

Historian John T. McNeill argues that 'in Celtic Brittany the church never bore great marks of distinction in learning, art, and heroic devotion such as we find in the church of Ireland and Britain'. It does, however, have another distinction. 'The rise of the Breton church', he says, 'was marked by the greatest individualism.' Past scholars of Celtic Christianity have noted that Celtic abbots in some ways took precedence over bishops. This has been overemphasized; bishops still held the power, but abbots usually set the agenda. In Brittany, however, the monastic priest often had neither abbot nor bishop watching over him. The archbishop of Tours occasionally made efforts to bring the churches and monasteries under uniform control, but he was repeatedly rebuffed. Other Frankish church leaders were later agitated by some differences in Celtic and continental practices. Again, the Celtic Christians seem to have disregarded many of these. It was apparently not out of obstinacy, but out of pragmatism. They simply believed that their practices were the way things were done.

'[For] the Irish people… the custom of travelling to foreign lands has now become almost second nature.'

WALAHFRID STRABO,
THE LIFE OF ST GALL

Columbanus, missionary to Europe

One monk who had several run-ins with the Frankish ecclesiastic rulers is also the monk who most exemplifies the self-exiling *peregrini*. His name was Columba, which has for centuries frustrated scholars and writers eager to distinguish this 'dove' from the founder of Iona. Some have designated him Columba the Younger, as he was born

around 543, about two decades after Iona's Colum
Cille (c. 521–97). Others have adopted the Irish name
Columbán. The Latin convention of referring to this
missionary exile as Columbanus seems most popular.

The peregrini were not mere pilgrims or wanderers.
They did not leave their home 'to find themselves' or in
search of some mystical place or spiritual relic. Nor were
they tourists; when peregrini left home, return would be an
unthinkable embarrassment. They were instead missionary
monks, driven by both the evangelistic zeal of Patrick
and the love of cloistered study. Perhaps no one vocalized
their goal as well as Columbanus, who said he sought 'the
salvation of many, and a solitary spot of my own'.

Columbanus's first hagiographer, Jonas, wrote a
mere 28 years after his subject's death in 613, almost
instantaneous when compared to other hagiographies.
And before that, Jonas had spent years interviewing
Columbanus's many companions. So he was probably
not exaggerating much, if at all, when he wrote that
Columbanus's 'fine figure, his splendid colour, and
his noble manliness made him beloved by all'. And in
such beauty lay the problem: 'He aroused... the lust of
lascivious maidens, especially of those whose fine figure
and superficial beauty are wont to enkindle mad desires
in the minds of wretched men.' As a young man, he feared
he was on the brink of giving in to such vain 'lusts of the
world', so he sought the guidance of a local female hermit.
'Away, O youth, away!' she advised. 'Flee from corruption,
into which, as you know, many have fallen.' Columbanus
left, shaken, to pack his things in preparation for a
monastic life. When he told his mother he was leaving,
she became so distraught she blocked the doorway. But
Columbanus was undeterred, 'leaping over both threshold
and mother'.

The exile did not immediately leave the island, but in
travelling from Leinster in eastern Ireland to the monastery
of Gleenish, in north-western County Fermanagh, home
must have seemed far off. He studied under an abbot named

Sinell and wrote a commentary on the psalms, but before long continued on to Bangor to study under Sinell's master, Comgall. For almost 25 years, Columbanus studied, prayed, fasted and lived the life of most Irish monks. There is no evidence that Columbanus was unhappy at Bangor, but by his mid-forties he began to feel that Ireland's north-eastern tip was not a distant enough exile. At first reluctant, Comgall allowed the exile and 12 companions (it was common for monks to deliberately emulate Jesus and his followers in such a manner) to exile themselves to Frankish Gaul.

They founded three monasteries in rapid succession – Annegray, Luxeuil and Fontaine – each one growing so quickly new ones had to be created. 'Modesty and moderation, meekness and mildness adorned them all in equal measure,' wrote Jonas. 'The evils of sloth and dissention were banished. Pride and haughtiness were expiated by severe punishments. Scorn and envy were driven out by faithful diligence. So great was the might of their patience, love and mildness that no one could doubt that the God of mercy dwelt among them.'

Such exemplary living attracted many of the new monks. And, Jonas says, others 'began to crowd about in order that they might recover their health and in order to seek aid in all their infirmities'. But Columbanus's monasteries also probably attracted potential Frankish monks because Irish monastic life, for all its severities, offered opportunities continental monasticism did not. As historian Richard Fletcher notes, 'its emphasis on the supervisory role of the abbot (perhaps a kinsman) of a monastic network – rather than, as previously, the local bishop – was reassuring to families who might be apprehensive, sometimes with justice, of the covetous designs of the nearby bishop of its endowments'.

Indeed, Columbanus had significant run-ins with the local bishops. To them, the Irishman was a schismatic with disregard for church supervision and potentially unorthodox beliefs (these focused especially over the celebration of Easter). To Columbanus, the bishops seemed arrogant and vain. Jonas probably echoes his subject's opinion when he blames 'the carelessness of the bishops' when he notes 'the Christian faith had almost departed from that country'. In 603 the bishops convened a synod at Chalon-sur-Saône to examine Columbanus. Whether he felt the synod was unimportant or whether he feared his often-hot temper would get the better of him in direct confrontation, he did not attend. Instead, he sent a letter that, while superficially friendly, contains some severe underlying criticism: 'I give thanks to my God that for my sake so many holy men have gathered together to treat the truth of faith and good works, and as, befits such, to judge of the matters under dispute with a just judgment, through senses sharpened to the discernment of good and evil,' he begins. Then the jab: 'Would that you did so more often!'

He repeatedly calls for them to be humble, and dismisses their complaints of theological malpractice. 'I am not the author of this difference,' he writes, 'and it is for the sake of Christ the Saviour… that I have entered these lands as a pilgrim.' He concludes by asking to continue his life as a stranger among them, and suggests that they love and pray for each other.

Columbanus's apparent disregard for the hierarchical conventions of continental Christianity did not simply apply to the local bishops. It was one thing to begin his letter to them, 'To the holy lords and fathers – or better, brothers – in Christ.' It was quite another to extend that attitude towards a medieval pope.

Nevertheless in a letter to Pope Boniface IV (608–15), Columbanus is not just unceremonious, he is casual, even making light-hearted puns. Of Boniface's predecessor, Vigilus, he riffs, 'Be vigilant, I implore you, pope, be vigilant and again I say be vigilant, since perhaps he who was called Vigilant was not vigilant.' Such a pun echoes an earlier, even more playful letter to Pope Gregory the Great (590–604), in which he used Ecclesiastes 9:4 to make a pun on Pope Leo's name: 'A living dog is better than a dead Leo [lion].'

And he is not unaware of his breaches of protocol. 'What makes me bold, if I may say so,' he wrote to Boniface, 'is partly the freedom of speech which is the custom of my country. For among us it is not the person but the argument that carries weight.'

Perhaps sensing that the bishops' questions over his orthodoxy would not be the last time he and his countrymen would be viewed with suspicion, Columbanus never misses an opportunity to assure Boniface of Ireland's adherence to the gospel. 'For all we Irish, inhabitants of the world's edge, are disciples of Saints Peter and Paul and of all the disciples who, by the Holy Spirit, wrote the divine Scripture,' he wrote to Pope Boniface. 'And we accept nothing outside the evangelical and apostolic teaching. Not one has been a heretic, not one a Judaizer, not one a schismatic, but the Catholic Faith as it was given to us first by you, that is the successors of the holy apostles, is preserved intact.' Sadly, he suggests, the same cannot necessarily be said of Rome. 'Just as your honour is great because of the dignity of your see, your must take great care not to lose your honour through some untowardness.'

'Going to Rome is lots of effort, little profit. You won't find the king there unless you take him along.'

ANCIENT IRISH
POEM

A double exile

But Columbanus's greatest political challenge would come not from Rome, but from his backyard. Brunhilde, a mercenary Visigothic princess, had become ruler of Burgundy after the assassination of her husband. Her son, Theuderic, had visted Luxeuil, but now found himself on the Irish monk's bad side. Theuderic had many concubines, who had borne him four sons. Grandmother Brunhilde was eager to ensure her line. By asking – or rather, demanding – that Columbanus bless the illegitimate heirs, she earned his wrath. He called the children sons of harlots and prophesied that they would never rise to power. It was a costly jeremiad. The monk was arrested and ordered 'to return to the place whence you came to this land'.

This horrified Columbanus. 'I do not think it would be

pleasing to my Creator if I should go back to the home which I left because of my love for Christ,' he argued. Nevertheless the voluntary exile became an involuntary exile from Burgundy. He and his fellow Irish monks were rounded up and escorted by military guard from Luxeuil through Besançon, Auexerre, Orleans, and Tours to Nantes, where he was placed aboard a ship bound for Ireland. Perhaps Columbanus was right. Maybe God really was not pleased with the idea of the impertinent Irishman being forced to return home. In any case, the ship bearing Columbanus and his companions ran aground shortly after embarking.

A 15th-century wall painting in the abbey library of St Gall depicts the town's namesake and his mentor, Columbanus, travelling across Lake Constance.

That he escaped was hardly a surprise. As he wrote when the guards came to put him aboard, 'If I escape there is no guard to prevent it; for they seem to desire this, that I should escape.'

Now free but a double exile, Columbanus seemed momentarily directionless. He and his companions travelled east to Metz, and though they met with a friendly reception, decided not to stay long. Instead, they headed up the Rhine to Bregenz, on the shore of Lake Constance in what is now Switzerland. It was likely on this journey that the monk wrote his famous 'Boat Song'. The shanty starts as a tribute to the boat and becomes a metaphor for the Christian life:

Cut in the forests, swept down the two-horned Rhine,
*   our keel, tight-caulked, now floats upon the sea.*
Ho, men! Let the echoes resound with our ho!
*   But manly strength has force to tame the storm.*
Ho, men! Let the echoes resound with our ho!

Firm faith and holy ardour conquer all.
*   The ancient fiend, defeated, breaks his arrows.*
Let your souls, men, remembering Christ, cry ho!

Switzerland was not to hold Columbanus for long, either. Now in his seventies, Columbanus began leading his companions over the Alps into Italy. His aim there was to convert the Arian Lombards, who had come to the country half a century earlier. But on the way, Columbanus's hot temper again flared. Gall, one of his most faithful disciples, became too ill to travel. Unconvinced, the elder demanded that his subordinate rise and walk. When Gall did not, Columbanus took a drastic measure. 'I enjoin on you before I go,' he proclaimed, 'that so long as I live in the body, you do not dare to celebrate Mass.'

While Gall stayed behind, the other Irishmen crossed into Italy. Passing through Milan, they built the first Italo-Irish monastery at Bobbio over the ruins of a church

supposedly founded by Peter. Though strong enough to
help in the monastery's construction, Columbanus did not
last long thereafter. Shortly before his death in November
613, he sent his staff of office north to Gall. Whether it
was an act of apology or forgiveness, it was clearly one of
reconciliation.

Columbanus's quantifiable legacy is among the
most impressive anywhere in church history. He and
his disciples founded at least 60 monasteries throughout
Europe, and were among the first to bring the passionate
Irish Christianity so deeply into the continent.

After Columbanus's death,
Gall seems to have somewhat
changed in his evangelistic
methods. When travelling with
his superior, both regularly
smashed pagan idols and threw
them in the lake. Among the
Alemanni around what is now
Switzerland, however, Gall's
efforts were more akin to those
of Patrick two centuries earlier,

The abbey in
Bobbio, Italy,
where
Columbanus
finished his
earthly travels.

gently urging conversion. Like those before him, he both
befriended the local rulers to assist in his efforts and took
the gospel to the homes of the less powerful. Gall was
apparently comfortable with those in power (befriending
a local duke, for example), but he avoided it for himself.
He refused an offer to become abbot of Luxeuil when
Columbanus's second successor died, and similarly turned
down the bishopric of Constance. Gall believed the bishop
of Constance should be a native of the country, so he
secured the appointment of one of his students, a German
named John. This student had led Gall into the wilds
near Lake Constance to find a secluded base. John tried
to warn Gall from assuming the area would be as monk-
friendly as Ireland, telling tales of ferocious wild animals
and even more ferocious weather. Gall turned a deaf ear to
the advice, deciding to create a hermitage at the first place

he fell. According to Gall's hagiographer, Walahfrid Strabo (who left us the story about the dispute between Gall and Columbanus; Jonas omitted it), John was right about the area's wild beasts. But under God's protection, Gall tamed them. One bear learned how to fetch the monk's firewood in exchange for a loaf of bread.

Gall preached at John's consecration as bishop, and his sermon is the only writing of his that survives (though a German phrase book may also be in his own hand). An even greater legacy, however, remains his monastery, which became one of the greatest of all medieval educational centres. It soon passed from a Celtic rule to the Benedictine Rule, but its library attracted scholars and saints from around the Christian world. By the time of Gall's death in 640, the Alemanni were almost totally Christian.

Fursa the visionary

Brendan's nephew, Fursa, was another famous peregrinus and reportedly one of the most popular preachers in Ireland. He grew up educated in one of his uncle's monasteries, Inchiquin Island, then left to create his own hermitage. Bede raves that Fursa 'was of noble Irish blood, and even more noble in mind than in birth, for from his boyhood he had not only read sacred books and observed monastic discipline, but as is fitting in saints, had also diligently practised all that he had learned'. Fursa, however, was no hermit, travelling around the island to preach. When he 'could no longer endure the crowds that thronged him', says Bede, Fursa 'made a vow to spend his life as a pilgrim for love of our Lord, and to go wherever God should call him'. The first place God called him was to East Anglia, where Fursa befriended King Sigebert I – one of the most Christian of all monarchs (he had been educated by Columbanus, founded schools, and eventually relinquished his title to become a monk). The king granted the monk an abandoned fort to use as a monastery, but ten years later Fursa decided to give up his administrative tasks to return to a more reclusive life. This too did not last long, as pagans from the Anglo-Saxon region of Mercia launched regular raids on the area. Fursa then decided to cross the southern sea into Normandy. He was well received by the town of Mayoc, which asked him to stay. He is still remembered there, but his stay was brief; he moved on to Neustria, where he founded a monastery near Paris, at Lagny on the Marne. In his mid-seventies, Fursa decided to return to England but died on the way. He was buried at the new church in the northern town of Péronne, where his brother Ultán served as bishop. Until its destruction by Vikings in 880, the church was known as Peronna Scottorum, Péronne of the Irish.

Throughout his life, Fursa experienced ecstatic visions. The first of these seems to have been a near-death experience: after days of praying and fasting in a cross-vigil (with arms extended), the saint had a major fever. Then, says his hagiographer, Fursa's feet went cold, his hands stiffened, and his soul left his body. In fact, several of Fursa's visions came at times of illness. Sometimes, says Bede, God told him 'to continue his diligent preaching of the word, and to maintain his accustomed vigils and prayers with indefatigable zeal'. Other visions were more graphic, and inspired generations of readers. Bede opts not to describe most of these, encouraging his readers to seek out Fursa's hagiography, which

… describes the deceitful cunning with which the devils misrepresented his actions, words, and even thoughts, as though they were recorded in a book; and it tells of the joyful and sorrowful things that he learned both from the angels and from the saints who appeared among the angels.

Having said this, Bede cannot resist retelling one of the stories. Lifted into the heavens by angels, Fursa looks back down at the earth and sees a gloomy valley with four fires in the air. The angels explain that the flames were falsehood, covetousness, discord and cruelty, but all four quickly merged and burst near the saint. Fursa was saved by this

'[In the tales of peregrini] we do not read of inner crises of decision; rather we get the impression of prompt and unhesitating response to a divine imperative.'

JOHN T. MCNEILL,
THE CELTIC CHURCHES

attack, but on his return to earth was scorched by a damned
soul whose clothing Fursa had worn after the man died.
'You lit this fire, so you were burned,' an angel explained.
'Had you not accepted property from one who died in his
sins, you would not have shared in his punishment.' Back
in his body and restored to health, Fursa's shoulder and jaw
retained the burn marks. This served not only to remind

Irish Christianity
was introduced
by Columba
to Iona, from
where it spread
southwards,
through England.
At around the
same time, Irish
monks brought
the faith back
into continental
Europe.

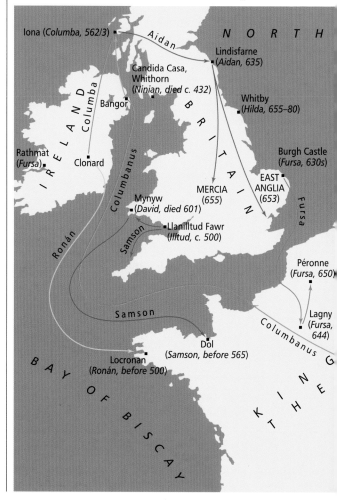

Iona (*Columba, 562/3*)

Aidan

N O R T H

Lindisfarne
• (*Aidan, 635*)

Candida Casa,
Whithorn
(*Ninian, died c. 432*)

Whitby
(*Hilda, 655–80*)

Bangor

B R I T A I N

I R E L A N D

Columba

Rathmat
(*Fursa*)

Clonard

Burgh Castle
(*Fursa, 630s*)

MERCIA
(655)

EAST
ANGLIA
(653)

Columbanus

Mynyw
• (*David, died 601*)

Fursa

•Llanilltud Fawr
(*Illtud, c. 500*)

Péronne
(*Fursa, 650*)

Samson

Ronán

Lagny
(*Fursa,
644*)

Columbanus

G

Samson

H

Dol
(*Samson, before 565*)

B
A
Y

Locronan
(*Ronán, before 500*)

K

T

H
E

O
F

B I S C A Y

Fursa to maintain his holy separation, but was also evidence for sceptics. Pope Martin I was reportedly one of these doubters, but upon seeing Fursa's scar fell on his knees and apologized. The Christian public, however, was not as sceptical. Fursa's visions circulated and were taken as divine revelations of the afterlife. They even reportedly became one of Dante Alighieri's inspirations for *The Divine Comedy*.

A flood of saints

So many Celtic saints emigrated to Brittany, Gaul, and beyond (monastic foundations were established in Spain, Norway, and other distant regions) that in 870 Henric of Auxerre wrote in his *Life of Germanus*, 'Almost all of Ireland, despising the sea, is migrating to our shores with a herd of philosophers.' By the mid-600s, Irish peregrini were already creating systems to care for their fellow exiles. One notable example is Fiacra, who set up a hospice near his monastery in Meaux. His legend tells how the local bishop promised the saint as much land as he could mark off with his spade in one day. As Fiacra began to dig, the ground miraculously opened up and marked off the territory for him. (The legend also tells of an angry woman who opposed Fiacra and eventually became both made of stone and the justification for banning women from the monastery.) Today Fiacra is remembered as

'The new invaders were unarmed white-robed monks with books in their satchels and psalms on their lips, seeking no wealth or comfort but only the opportunity to preach and to pray.'

JOHN T. MCNEILL,
THE CELTIC CHURCHES

the patron saint of gardeners. He is also remembered for two less auspicious namesakes: French cabs (four-wheeled cabs premiered in 1620 outside Paris's Hôtel Saint-Fiacre) and St Fiacre's Disease (haemorrhoids).

One of the Celtic lands' most renowned missionaries was not a Celt at all. Boniface (680–754) was an Anglo-Saxon born in Devonshire (his birthname was Wynfrith or Winfrid). He had spent time as a monk, but his mission to Germany in 719 was not one of peregrini. It was a mission directed by Pope Gregory II, who wanted Boniface not only to convert the heathen (those 'not yet cleansed by the waters of holy Baptism'), but to suppress the heretics (those 'led astray… and now serve idols under the guise of the Christian religion'). 'You seem to glow with the salvation-bringing fire which our Lord came to send upon the earth,' Gregory told him. Indeed, Boniface was full of fire, smashing idols, cutting down sacred trees, and demanding that heretical missionaries not only be excommunicated but imprisoned in solitary confinement. Freelance missionary monks had no place in his plan to organize the church. He was not always hostile to Celtic Christians – an Irishman named Abel, for example, was appointed to the See of Rheims – but many were condemned, even those in the Roman hierarchy. The bishop of Salzburg, a Celt named Virgil, was attacked for postulating 'that there are another world and other men under the earth, and another sun and moon'. 'Wandering bishops', meanwhile, were to Boniface's mind some kind of freakish, subhuman creature akin to the mythic centaurs. They were not quite heretical, but they were schismatic. By the time Boniface died, the church around what is now Germany – re-energized largely by the Celtic peregrini – was far more organized and controlled. Peregrini continued to flow in from the north, and were sought out for their knowledge for centuries to come. But the height of their influence over northern Europe was over.

Resurrection and Raids

A n apocryphal legend says that Pope Gregory the Great, before he became pope, once came upon a merchant selling young slave boys. Having never seen such a fair-haired and fair-skinned race before, Gregory asked where they came from. 'They come from Britain,' he was told, 'where all the people have this appearance.' Not all did. These were not children of Celtic descent but Angles, descendants of the tribes that had migrated to England from southern Jutland (modern Denmark and northern Germany) in the 5th century. Gregory misheard the name of their race. 'That is an appropriate name,' he said, 'for they have faces like angels and it is right that they should become fellow-heirs with the angels in heaven.' Gregory reportedly begged the pope to send him to England, but was refused. When he took the papacy, however, he was quick to make sure that England received missionaries.

In 596, Pope Gregory sent Augustine and 40 monks under him to convert England. They had all been trained in Gregory's Roman monastery, and Augustine himself was an expert in theology, monasticism and management. Unfortunately, he was also arrogant. Arriving in Britain, he immediately chastised the local clergy for preferring 'their own customs to those in universal use among Christian churches'. Wondering what to do, seven British bishops and other monks, mainly from Bangor, consulted a 'wise and prudent hermit'.

'If he is a man of God, follow him,' the monk advised. 'If Augustine is meek and lowly of heart, it shows that he

'From a Celtic perspective, calling Augustine of Canterbury "the Apostle of England" has much in common with naming the New World for Amerigo Vespucci.'

RICHARD J. WOODS,
*THE SPIRITUALITY OF
THE CELTIC SAINTS*

bears the yoke of Christ himself, and offers it to you. But if he is haughty and unbending, then he is not of God, and you should not listen to him.'

The troubled clergy wanted more specifics. How would Augustine demonstrate meekness or haughtiness? 'If he rises courteously as you approach, rest assured that he is the servant of Christ and do as he asks,' the hermit answered. 'But if he ignores you and does not rise, then, since you are

Bede believed his history continued the New Testament story. Visitors to the monastery at Wearmouth and Jarrow can still see what is supposedly the historian's chair, depicted here in this English manuscript illumination from the late 12th century.

in the majority, do not comply with his demands.' Augustine
did not rise. Instead, he made demands, prophesying
that if he was not obeyed, the English would kill the local
clerics. 'And, as though by divine judgment, all these things
happened as Augustine foretold,' recounts Bede, noting a
battle that killed 1,200 monks – most from Bangor.

Actually, everything recounted so far in this chapter
comes from Bede, the Anglo-Saxon historian known as
the father of English church history. He is a partisan for
the Romans and Anglo-Saxons, but he repeatedly praises
Celtic Christians for their holiness. 'The Venerable Bede
is often portrayed as an apologist for Roman Christianity
and as one of the chief architects for the notion of
Englishness,' writes modern historian Ian Bradley,
'I firmly believe that he was also largely responsible for
initiating the British, and more especially the English,
love affair with "Celtic" Christianity.'

The trouble with Easter

Bede's objectivity is brought under the greatest scrutiny
when he discusses the differences between the way Celtic
and Roman churches calculated Easter. Though this may
seem trivial to modern Christians – who may not even
know that there is still a difference between Western and
Eastern calendars, but for different reasons – to early
medieval believers it was terribly important. As early
as 314 the Council of Arles, where British bishops were
among the delegates, begged Pope Sylvester to 'write
immediately to all, giving directions on this observance,
so that it may be celebrated by us on the same day and at
the same time throughout the world'.

The difference in calculation comes from the
difference between a solar year and 12 lunar months
(used in determining Jewish festivals like Passover). The
earth revolves around the sun every 12.3683 months – so
the ancients decided to add an extra lunar month every so
often to balance the scales. The Celts threw in 31 months
every 84 years (leaving them only 0.0007 of an extra

month) while the Roman church added 7 months every 19 years (only 0.0001 months over). The controversy was not just astronomical, however. Theology played a much more important role.

Only a few years after the Council of Arles, the Council of Nicea became one of the most important meetings of church history. Foremost among the agenda items was the suppression of the Arians, who believed Jesus was not fully God. But the council also condemned (as schismatics, not heretics) a lesser-known group called the Quartodecimans, a Christian sect that celebrated Easter at the Jewish Passover, whether it fell on a Sunday or not. Another group of Christians had so strongly opposed such ties with Judaism that they did not want to celebrate Easter on Sunday if it *did* coincide with the Passover. Others queried whether Good Friday or Easter Sunday should be associated with the Jewish Passover. Arguments over Easter even hinged on when the day began – at sunrise, sunset, or at some other time? And then there was the issue of the vernal equinox and the symbolism that came with it – at the equinox, day becomes longer than night just as Christ, the Light of the World, conquered the Prince of Darkness in his resurrection.

For early medieval Christians, taking all these matters into account was no game. 'What was at stake was the harmony between human and divine law,' historian Thomas O'Loughlin writes in his book *Celtic Theology*. 'God had created the universe in an orderly and numbered way; everywhere its order was a testimony to the ideas in the mind of God as he created, and to see these patterns in the material creation was to see beyond matter into the divine purposes.' Celtic Christians, Roman Christians, Eastern Christians, and the rest of the early Christian world believed the statement in Wisdom 11:20 that God 'arranged all things in measure, number and weight'. Jesus was clear that the time of his death and resurrection was divinely appointed. 'The hour has come,' he said repeatedly. How wrong it would be, then, to commemorate his resurrection haphazardly.

Many recent historians have downplayed the Easter controversy, saying either that it was simply a manifestation of the battle between Celtic religious autonomy and the hierarchical Roman church, or that it has been greatly exaggerated due to Bede's strong interest in the subject. The controversy, however, appears throughout the history of the Celtic churches. It was apparently a main source of controversy between Columbanus and the provincial religious leaders around Luxeuil, and Columbanus himself worried over the dispute. 'The dangers I mean are the dangers of disagreement,' he wrote to his monastery just before boarding his ill-fated ship back to Ireland. 'I fear lest there be disagreement on account of Easter, lest perhaps, through the Devil's tricks, [the community's enemies] wish to divide you, if you do not keep peace with them; for now, without me, you seem to stand less firmly there.'

Were the Celts insubordinate?
Columbanus may have been too informal with popes, even sometimes critical, but he was no Martin Luther. Despite the histories of those trying to draw a line connecting the Celtic churches to Protestantism, Columbanus appears to have bent the knee to Rome. Still, elsewhere Columbanus's letter suggests that he had heard the method Rome used to compute Easter and the reasons for it, but ultimately disagreed. This frustrated Augustine's successor at Canterbury, Laurence, who in 605 questioned Columbanus's claim that he and his fellow Irish preserved the Catholic faith wholly intact. 'When the apostolic see sent us, according to its custom, to preach to pagan peoples in these western lands, and in the whole world, we entered this island which is called Britain,' he said in a letter to Irish Christians. 'Before we learnt the truth, we believed that the Britons and the Irish followed the custom of the

universal Church, and so we held both in veneration. When we came to know the Britons, we believed the Irish to be superior. We learnt, however, from… the abbot Columbanus in Gaul, that the Irish do not differ at all from the Britons in their way of life.'

Twenty-three years after Laurence's letter to the Irish, another missive came – this time from Pope Honorius himself. 'He earnestly warned them not to imagine that their little community, isolated at the uttermost ends of the earth, had a monopoly of wisdom over all the ancient and new churches throughout the world,' Bede records. 'And he asked them not to keep a different Easter, contrary to the calculations and synodical decrees of all the bishops of the world.'

This argument that the entire world apart from Britain and Ireland celebrated Easter one way may have been more persuasive than the mere fact that the request came from Rome. That question, however, is mired in centuries of arguments between Protestant and Catholic historians. For Cummian, who was probably the abbot of Darrow, the two issues were inextricably united. 'What can be felt worse for Mother Church than to say, "Rome is mistaken, Jerusalem is mistaken, Alexandria is mistaken, Antioch is mistaken, the Scots and Britons alone have sound wisdom."' Those opposing the change, he said, were 'an insignificant group of Britons and Irish who are almost at the end of the world, and, if I may say so, but pimples on the face of the earth'.

In the household of King Oswy of Northumbria, dating differences led to more practical tensions. The king kept to the Celtic date, while his wife, Eanfled, followed the Romans. 'It is said,' Bede writes, 'that the confusion in those days was such that Easter was kept twice in one year, so that when the King had ended Lent and was keeping Easter, the Queen and her attendants were still fasting and keeping Palm Sunday.' Family conflict intensified when Oswy's son, Aldfrith, switched sides and became a vocal supporter of the Roman date.

The tonsure

'There was no small argument about this as well,' Bede writes over differences in the tonsure – a sacred shearing of hair when taking clerical vows. The Roman tonsure was a shaved circle on the top of the head. Though it had only been around for about two centuries by Bede's time, the Anglo-Saxon historian believed it dated back to the apostle Peter, who first shaved his head in such a manner to resemble Christ's crown of thorns. 'Therefore we who desire to be saved by Christ's Passion like Peter wear this sign of the Passion on the crown of the head, which is the highest part of the body,' Bede wrote. The tonsure, he believed, gave 'constant protection against the assaults of wicked spirits, and serve[d] as a continual reminder that he must crucify the flesh with all its vices and evil desires'.

By the time this image was painted in the early 13th century, the Celtic tonsure had disappeared.

Celtic clergy, meanwhile, shaved a line on their head 'from ear to ear' and everything in front of it, allowing their hair to grow in the back (they may have also left a fringe above the forehead). Some historians suggest this may have been a practice of the druids, but Bede and others believed it came from Simon Magus, the Samaritan magician who tried to offer the early apostles money in exchange for the supernatural power of the Holy Spirit. 'I ask what faithful Christian will not instantly detest it, and reject it together with all his magic,' Bede said. But Bede admits that 'the apostles were not all tonsured in the same manner', and Celtic Christians probably associated their tonsure with the apostle John. Much to the consternation of Bede and others, some Celts who accepted the Roman date for Easter still wore the Celtic tonsure, including Adomnán.

The Synod of Whitby

With pressure building on all sides, in 664 Oswy called for both parties to meet and settle their differences. They chose to meet at the double monastery of Streanaeshalch, founded by Hilda, 'a woman devoted to God' according to Bede. Though Anglo-Saxon (a member of the Angle royal family, in fact), Hilda was Celtic in practice and spiritual pedigree. A student of Aidan of Lindisfarne, she gained prominence both as spiritual adviser and an administrator of monasteries at Streanaeshalch (now better known by the name later Danes gave it: Whitby) and Hartlepool. 'So great was her prudence that not only ordinary folk, but kings and princes used to come and ask her advice in their difficulties,' writes Bede. Everyone who knew her called her Mother – a designation apparently not universal among abbesses.

Hilda sided with the Celtic Easter date, but she served as host rather than disputant. That role fell to the Irish bishop of Lindisfarne, Colmán. 'The Easter customs which I observe were taught me by my superiors, who sent me here as a bishop,' he began. 'And all our forefathers, men beloved of God, are known to have observed these customs.' Colmán also argued, based on an ancient document known as the *Liber Anatolii*, that the apostle John himself – 'the disciple especially loved by our Lord' – had used their method for Easter dating. (Unfortunately for the Celts, the Quartodecimans had also appealed to John's Easter practices to defend themselves. Even more unfortunately, the *Liber Anatolii* was a forgery and a fraud.)

Scheduled to argue for the Roman date was Agilbert, a Frankish bishop who later became bishop of Paris. He, however, was reluctant to argue through the interpreter, a Celtic bishop named Cedd. Agilbert may have been particularly sensitive to language issues around Anglo-Saxon royalty. Years earlier, Agilbert had served as bishop in Wessex. Unfortunately, Bede records, 'the king, who understood only Saxon, grew tired of the bishop's foreign

'Perhaps no one did more to foster this impression of a vanished golden age than the historian through whose eyes all subsequent generations have viewed the Whitby debate. The Venerable Bede...'

IAN BRADLEY,
CELTIC CHRISTIANITY: MAKING MYTHS AND CHASING DREAMS

speech, and invited to the province a bishop of his own tongue'. Perhaps not wishing likewise to bore King Oswy, Agilbert asked that his protégé, a priest named Wilfrid, take his place. It was a smart move. Wilfrid was not just eloquent, he was passionate; he had only recently renounced the Celtic date for the Roman one as a student at Canterbury.

'Our Easter customs are those that we have seen universally observed in Rome,' Wilfrid began, appealing to apostles Peter and Paul over John. 'We have also seen the same customs generally observed throughout Italy and Gaul… [and] in Africa, Asia, Egypt, Greece, and throughout the world wherever the church of Christ has spread. The only people who are stupid enough to disagree with the whole world are these Scots and their obstinate adherents the Picts and Britons, who inhabit only a portion of these two islands in the remote ocean.' Furthermore, Wilfrid argued, if the Celts really were following John they would have joined the Quartodecimans in celebrating Easter on whatever day of the week Passover fell on – Sunday or not. 'You conform neither to John nor Peter, the law nor the gospel, in your keeping of our greatest festival,' he concluded.

Again Colmán tried to appeal to his own traditions and forefathers. 'Are we to believe that our most revered Father Columba and his successors, men so dear to God, thought or acted contrary to Holy Scripture when they followed this custom?' he asked rhetorically. 'The holiness of many of them is confirmed by heavenly signs, and their virtues by miracles; and having no doubt that they are saints, I shall never cease to emulate their lives, customs, and discipline.'

At this, Wilfrid became even more acrimonious, quoting Matthew 7:22–23. 'I can only say that when many shall say to our Lord at the day of judgment: "Have we not prophesied in thy name, and cast out devils, and done many wonderful works?" the Lord will reply, "I never knew you."' This is not to say that Columba and all the

other Celtic saints were burning in hell, Wilfrid assured
his listeners, but they were certainly mistaken. They did
not know any better, Wilfrid suggested. Colmán and his
ilk, meanwhile, were in danger of damnation by rejecting
correction. He asked:

*For although your Fathers were holy men, do you imagine
that they, a few men in a corner of a remote island, are to be
preferred before the universal church of Christ throughout
the world? And even if your Columba – or, may I say, yours if
he was the servant of Christ – was a saint potent in miracles,
can he take precedence before the most blessed Prince of the
Apostles, to whom our Lord said: 'Thou art Peter, and upon
this rock I will build my church… and to thee I will give the
keys of the kingdom of heaven'?*

When Oswy heard this, the debate was over. Is it true, he
asked Colmán, that Jesus gave Peter the keys to heaven,
and that Columba had no such authority? The Irish bishop
acknowledged this reading of Matthew 16:18. 'Then, I tell
you, Peter is the guardian of the gates of heaven, and I
shall not contradict him,' Oswy declared. 'Otherwise, when
I come to the gates of heaven, he who holds the keys may
not be willing to open them.'

Oswy was not alone in his decision. Many leaders of
Celtic churches and monasteries began observing Easter
with the Romans, including Hilda and Cedd. But not
Colmán. He left Lindisfarne and returned (with the relics
of Aidan) to Iona, which continued to observe Columba's
calendar for another 150 years. After a few years on Iona,
Colmán and several of his followers returned to Ireland,
settling on the island's western shores.

Through the years, largely as a result of Bede's writing,
the so-called Synod of Whitby was seen as the turning
point of Celtic church history – the moment that the
Romans succeeded in their (depending on your point of
view) oppression or correction. It was a pivotal moment,
but not on such a grand scale. The meeting marked the

end of Iona's ecclesiastic influence over Northumbria (though Northumbrian youth continued to flock to Celtic monasteries), but not the end of Celtic Christianity or the triumph of the Roman church. For one thing, more than half of Ireland had already accepted the Roman Easter dates by the 664 meeting at Streanaeshalch. For another, Oswy was a local king and held little real power over church observances.

Those looking for a more direct confrontation on behalf of Rome can jump ahead another 16 years, to the Synod of Hertford in 672. Wilfrid was there, but the most disdain for the Celtic church seems to have come from Theodore, the archbishop of Canterbury. He believed the Celts to be heretics and schismatics, and the synod's resolutions reflect these beliefs. They not only firmly set down the Roman dating of Easter, but also outlawed monks wandering 'from place to place'. Failure to conform meant excommunication and thus eternal damnation.

Even this decree did not convince everyone. Adomnán, the abbot of Iona and hagiographer of Columba, converted to the Roman reforms around the year 690. This move, Bede records, set him against his disciples. 'On his return home, he tried to lead his own people in Iona and those who were under the jurisdiction of that monastery into the correct ways he had learned and wholeheartedly accepted, but in this he failed.' He had more success during visits to Ireland, reportedly convincing the Irish who were not already using the Roman Easter to accept it, which they did at the Synod of Birr (where they also adopted Adomnán's Law of Innocents). Adomnán returned to Iona and again tried to convince the monks to change their calendar, but again they refused. Before either side could celebrate the next Easter and widen the schism between abbot and monk, Adomnán had died.

The monks of Iona, among the last to accept the Roman reforms, eventually did so around the year 716. It was ultimately not any force from Rome or decree from

Canterbury that eventually won them over, but the patient encouragement of a monk named Egbert. 'Being a most persuasive teacher who most faithfully practised all that he taught, he was given a ready hearing by everyone,' Bede says, 'and by his constant and devout exhortations he weaned them from the obsolete traditions of their ancestors.' Egbert himself died on Easter Sunday – the Roman one – 729. Iona was not the last of the hold-outs. Bede laments that even at the time of his writing in 731, the Britons in Wales 'still remain obdurate and crippled by their errors, going about with heads improperly tonsured, and keeping Christ's solemnity without fellowship with the Christian Church'. A few hold-outs also remained at Iona, where they were allowed to maintain their tonsure and calendar until the schism ended quietly in 767.

The fury of the Northmen

Before the end of the century, Iona had a new challenge – the Vikings. They first attacked Columba's island in 795, looting the church, dormitories and other buildings. In 802, they returned, but this time, they were not content to merely rob the buildings of their possessions; they burned the structures themselves to the ground. Four years later, they returned again, murdering 86 monks. The abbot could take no more raids, and the attacks had broken communication between Iona and its daughter monasteries. Oversight was moved from such a precarious island to Kells. With the seat went the relics of Columba, entombed in a gold and silver shrine. Other monks stayed at Iona. They knew the potential consequences, and some even looked forward to them. One of these was Blathmac, an Irishman who had renounced his royal upbringing and had become an abbot in Ireland. He was not the abbot of Iona, but he knew where Columba's bones were buried. And that was information that the Vikings, who returned on 19 January 825, wanted to know. Blathmac refused to reveal the location, and (after celebrating Mass) was slowly hacked to death on the steps of the altar. After this

'When the Norse first appeared solely as raiders from the sea and were quite external to Irish society, they were regarded as a horror in Ireland, more for their heathenism than for their piracy.'

MÁIRE AND
LIAM DE PAOR,
*EARLY CHRISTIAN
IRELAND*

tragedy, Iona's story is less clear. But raids continued against the monastery, even as late as 986.

Iona was an early target, but not the first. In 791, the Scandinavian raiders hit both northern England and northern Scotland. Two years later, the *Anglo-Saxon Chronicle*'s entry is dismal:

In this year dire forewarnings came over the land of the Northumbrians and miserably terrified the people; these were extraordinary whirlwinds and lightnings, and fiery dragons were seen flying in the air. A great famine soon followed these omens and soon after that, in the same year, the havoc of heathen men miserably destroyed God's church on Lindisfarne.

The Monymusk Reliquary, from the 8th century, reportedly held one of Columba's finger bones.

When word of the raid reached Alcuin in Aachen, he was horrified – even though he had never been to Lindisfarne himself. 'Behold the church of the holy Cuthbert bespattered with the blood of God's priests, robbed of all its ornaments, the most venerable place in all Britain given over as prey to the pagans,' he said.

The *Annals of Ulster* are no happier, noting in the

The majestic *Chi-Rho* illumination that begins Matthew 1:18 in the *Book of Kells*.

The *Book of Kells*

Sometime around the move from Iona to Kells, work began on the famous *Book of Kells*, one of the Celtic world's most beautiful artworks. Its 12-by-9-inch pages record the biblical Gospels, but more importantly, they illustrate them. 'Here you can look upon the face of the divine majesty drawn in a miraculous way,' historian Giraldus Cambrensis wrote in the late 1100s upon seeing the book.

If you take the trouble to look very closely, and penetrate with your eyes to the secrets of the artistry, you will notice such intricacies, so delicate and subtle, so close together, so well-knitted, so involved and bound together, and so fresh in their colourings, that you will not hesitate to declare that all of these things must have been the result of the work, not of men, but of angels.

The Annals of Ulster call it 'the most precious object in the Western world', but may have been referring to its gold cover and binding rather than the amazing ornamentation inside the book. Sometimes the artwork is holy, portraying a thin, golden-haired Jesus or a long-faced evangelist with a thick beard. At other times, human figures engage in more everyday activities; a man strangles a chicken, two other men wrestle and grab each other's beards. Animals – including cats, lizards, moths and deer – are also common. Some of the book's most amazing artwork, however, is merely abstract or symbolic, such as its full-page decoration of the chi-rho symbol. Sadly, the book remains unfinished, perhaps due to more Viking raids. Though it escaped direct assault for centuries, in 1007 raiders finally seized the book, tore off its valuable covers, and buried the rest under a sod. Three months later, it was recovered, and it now sits in Dublin's Trinity College.

same year 'the burning of Rechrann by heathens and Skye was overwhelmed and laid waste'. The story got worse in the following year's entry: 'Devastation of all the islands in Britain by heathens.' By 795, Vikings were raiding both Ireland's east and west coasts.

'From the fury of the Northmen, O Lord, deliver us,' Celtic monks prayed, but the fury continued. At first, the Vikings were content to merely attack from their Scandinavian homelands during an annual raiding season, from May to September. In the margin of a 9th-century manuscript, a monk issues a literary sigh of relief:

Fierce and wild is the wind tonight,
  it tosses the tresses of the sea to white;
on such a night as this I take my ease;
  fierce Northmen only course the quiet seas.

When raiders had to come over such a distance, the most susceptible targets were outlying islands. Iona was not as dangerous as the Hebrides (once Irish, but renamed 'the islands of the foreigners' within a century of the first Viking raids) and the even more distant Faroes. 'For nearly a hundred years hermits sailing from our country, Ireland, have lived [in the Faroes],' wrote the Irish scholar Dícuil in his 825 work, *Book on the Measurement of the World*. 'But just as they were always deserted from the beginning of the world, so now, because of the Northman pirates, they are emptied of anchorites [religious hermits], and filled with countless sheep and many diverse kinds of seabirds.'

By the 830s, however, the entire year was the raiding season, and just about everywhere was a target. In Ireland, only Connaught escaped the worst of the attacks. By then, the Vikings had apparently taken control of the Isle of Man, allowing them to attack anywhere in the Irish Sea with little warning. The Scandinavian pirates hit Armagh, long seen as the heart of Patrick's legacy, taking the abbot and Patrick's relics. Amazingly, both were returned within a year, after what was surely a huge ransom.

From saint-killers to saints

Historian John T. McNeill argues that the first Viking raid on a
Celtic monastery was not in 793, but 617. 'Sea rovers, possibly
at the instigation of a local enemy' fell upon Donnan (an Irish
friend and disciple of Columba) and his 53 monks on the island
of Eigg. The marauders allowed the monks to celebrate the
Easter Mass, then slaughtered each of them.

Encounters with Celtic Christians on remote British islands,
however, would eventually help to convert the Vikings to
Christianity. In the Scilly Isles off Land's End, a young Norwegian
named Olaf Trygvesson encountered a Cornish hermit with
prophetic gifts. 'Thou wilt become a renowned king and do
celebrated deeds,' the hermit told him.
'And that thou not doubt the truth of
this answer, listen to this.'
He then described
how Olaf's men
would attempt to
mutiny, and that
Olaf would be
wounded, carried to
his ship on a shield,
recover, and become
a Christian.

**A Norwegian ship
post from around
AD 850, about the
time the Vikings
had settled in
the British Isles.**

'Many men wilt
thou bring to faith and
baptism,' the prophet
said, 'and both to thy
own and others' good.'
When everything happened just as the hermit had said, Olaf
quickly returned to the island for baptism. Then he set off
to convert his homeland by force, saying 'All Norway will be
Christian or die.'

In 839, Vikings established their first winter camp in Ireland, on Lough Neagh. Such settlements allowed them, in the *Annals of Ulster*'s words, to 'plunder the peoples and churches of the north of Ireland', and take 'captive bishops and priests and scholars'. According to later legend-makers, about this same time the raiders became organized under the Viking leader Turgesius, who came with a 'great royal fleet' to northern Ireland and 'assumed the sovereignty of all the foreigners in Ireland'. Turgesius was not just interested in wealth – he sought colonization and total dominion over the islands. According to the legends, he also wanted to replace the islands' Christianity with the worship of Thor, Odin and other Norse gods. He even reportedly took the abbacy of Armagh and put his own wife in charge of the majestic monastery of Clonmacnoise, where she replaced Christian prayers with pagan oracles at the high altar.

While Norwegian invaders continued pillaging from Ireland's north, Danes dominated the south. They were no less ruthless. 'The whole of Munster… was plundered by them,' says *The Wars of the Gaedhil and the Gail*:

They made spoil-land, and sword-land and conquered land of her, throughout her land and generally; and they ravaged her chieftainries and her privileged churches and her sanctuaries; and they rent her shrines and her reliquaries and her books… In short, until the sand of the sea, or the grass of the field, or the starts of heaven are counted, it will not be easy to recount… what the Gaedhill… suffered from them.

The chronicler also recalls 'immense floods and countless sea-vomitings of ships and boats and fleets so that there was not a harbour nor a land-port nor a dún nor a fortress nor a fastness… without floods of Danes and pirates'. With so many pirates eager for booty, it was inevitable that conflict would arise between parties. The White Heathen and the Black Heathen, as the Norwegians and

The Irish town of Kells, in County Meath, continues to display ancient Celtic crosses among residents.

Viking raiders
initially plundered
the monasteries
of their treasures
and terrorized
the local people,
but eventually
they settled
and became
integrated into
Irish and British
society.

'When the
Vikings were
vanquished
in the early
eleventh
century,
Irish society
recovered, in
the sense that
the normal
business of life
sprang back in
its expectable
patterns. But
Ireland would
never recover
its cultural
leadership of
European
civilization.
It had been
marginalized
once more.'

THOMAS CAHILL,
*HOW THE IRISH
SAVED CIVILIZATION*

Danes were respectively called by the Irish, warred
among themselves. Perhaps the Irish would have been
able to take advantage of this – or unify against the
Vikings in some other way – but they too were torn
apart by tribal dissention. The Vikings had attacked
and demolished monasteries, but they were not the
first. The *Annals of Ulster* record 'a battle between the
communities of Clonmacnoise and Birr' in 760. Six
years later, Clonmacnoise battled again, this time with
Durrow – more than 200 died in the raid. In 775, there is
'a skirmish at Clonard between Donnchad [king of Tara]
and the community of Clonard'. Some historians even
argue that the violence among Irish tribes was already so
bad that the Viking raids had little real impact on society.

The legends credit Turgesius and his men with
founding Dubh-linn (black pool) and other permanent
camps in 841. Raids decreased as the Vikings started
demanding tribute and taxes. (The most horrible of which
may have been the Danes' nose tax – they demanded an
ounce of silver for each Irish nose. Those who did not
pay the price lost their nose.) With such settlement, the
landscape began to change. The Irish forts became places
of international trade – and Ireland's first real cities.
No longer were monasteries the dominant demographic
landmark. Eventually, the Northmen integrated into Irish
society, intermarrying and even accepting Christianity.
One prime example is Anlaf Curran, Olaf the Red. The
Norwegian ruler controlled Northumbria for 12 years,
but was later overthrown, then defeated again as head of
Dublin. In 970 Anlaf had raided the monastery at Kells. In
980, he died a monk of Iona, and was given a royal burial
there. Seven other Norwegian kings were also buried on
the holy island (along with 48 Scottish kings and four Irish
ones).

The Christianity of the Celts survived. But with Norse,
Angles, Saxons, Normans, and other foreigners pressing
in on the islands from all sides, the image becomes ever
more blurred. Irish Christians would still be sought for

Norwegian raids

Danish raids

Relics of Columba moved
from Iona to Kells, 806

Fortified Viking base
(*longphort*)

N O R T H

S E A

S C O T I A

Eigg, possible
Viking raid 617

Iona, raided
795, 802,
806, 825

Dumbarton,
sacked from
Dublin, 870/1

Lindisfarne,
raided 793

STRATHCLYDE

Jarrow,
raided 794

NORTHUMBRIA

Lough Neagh,
first winter base
in Ireland, 839

Annagassan

I R E L A N D

*Lough
Ree*

Kells

Isle of Man,
under Viking
control by 830

LINDSEY

Dublin,
founded c. 841

Limerick

Arklow

W A L E S

M E R C I A

EAST
ANGLIA

Wexford

Waterford

Cork

Youghal

London

Rochester

W E S S E X

CORNWALL

their learning, knowledge and skills, but the 'golden age' of Celtic Christianity – if there ever was such a thing – was over. This, however, would not stop Christians from trying to recapture its essence over the next millennium.

Celtic Christianity of the Non-Celts

I n 1995, Thomas Cahill took Celtic Christians to the American best-seller list. *How the Irish Saved Civilization* spent more than a year as one of the top-selling non-fiction books in the United States. Retelling the tales of Patrick, Columba, Columbanus and other Irish saints, Cahill's book described how holy scholars returned faith and knowledge to the European continent after the invasion of barbarian hordes:

As the Roman empire fell, as all through Europe matted, unwashed barbarians descended on the Roman cities, looting artifacts and burning books, the Irish, who were just learning to read and write, took up the great labour of copying all of Western literature – everything they could get their hands on. These scribes then served as conduits through which the Greco-Roman and Judeo-Christian cultures were transmitted to the tribes of Europe, newly settled amid the rubble and ruined vineyards they had overwhelmed. Without this Service of the Scribes, everything that happened subsequently would have been unthinkable. Without the Mission of the Irish Monks, who single-handedly refounded European civilization throughout the continent in the bays and valleys of their exile, the world that came after them would have been an entirely different one – a world without books. And our own world would never have come to be.

Several scholars dismissed Cahill's approach as too enthusiastic, too black-and-white, and bad history. 'This dream has had a pernicious effect on studies of the early

Irish church,' wrote Thomas O'Loughlin in his book *Celtic Theology*. 'For it has turned that study into a search for the peculiar, the unique and bizarre: what is common between that culture and the rest of Christendom becomes invisible, and what seems jarring becomes the norm.' Indeed, in his enthralling and descriptive book, Cahill admits he has tipped his journalistic scales in favour of 'many entertainers, persons of substance who have their story to tell, some of whom believe that their story is all there is to tell'. But he does so, he says, because the story of how the Irish saved civilization has gone untold. 'Many historians fail to mention it entirely, and few advert to the breathtaking drama of this cultural cliffhanger,' he writes. The subtitle of his book, in fact, is *The Untold Story of Ireland's Heroic Role from the Fall of Rome to the Rise of Medieval Europe*.

Continuing Celtic curiosity
The story of Celtic Christians and their contributions to the world was not, however, buried during the Viking raids like the *Book of Kells*, only to be dug up and recovered at the end of the last century. Ever since Adomnán and Bede, historians and scholars have been fascinated by the lives of these Celtic Christians and have portrayed them as saintly heroes. Ian Bradley sees at least six different Celtic Christian revivalist movements in the last millennium and a half. However, Bradley writes in *Celtic Christianity: Making Myths and Chasing Dreams*, 'their leading protagonists have generally, although not exclusively, been non-Celts. From the Anglo-Saxon Bede and the Anglo-Norman chroniclers of the 13th century to the predominantly English enthusiasts in the van of the current revival, it has largely been outsiders who have identified a distinctive "Celtic" strain of Christianity and found it particularly attractive.'

The first revival, Bradley says, came from hagiographers, whose emphasis was generally on proving the holiness and power of the specific saints they were writing about. Often, as we have seen, this was for political purposes. The saints, however, were seen as more than excuses for worldly control, they were exemplars. The hagiographers, as well as historians like Bede, saw the Celtic saints of the 400s and 500s as being pure and pious – unlike the decadence, corruption and worldliness they saw in their own day. For example, Bede writes about Aidan of Lindisfarne, 'His life is in marked contrast to the apathy of our own times, for all who accompanied him, whether monks or lay-folk, were required to meditate, that is, either to read the Scriptures or to learn the Psalms.'

The second revival began after the Battle of Hastings, as the Norman conquest brought England, Scotland, Wales, and even Ireland under English control. Ironically, the strongest passion for the golden age saints did not come from the conquered desperate to cling to their cultural identity, but from the conquerors. 'Undoubtedly there was a strong element of opportunism and good public relations in this pro-Celtic approach,' Bradley writes. 'It cast the victors of the Norman Conquest in the role of consolidators and continuers of native tradition rather than as unfeeling aliens out to destroy all that they came across.'

Not that they *were* unfeeling aliens, of course. One of these foreigners was Queen Margaret, Scotland's first canonized saint. The descendant of English princes, her father fled to Hungary after the Dane Canute the Great took the throne of England. Her mother was a Bavarian princess whose father, St Stephen, had recently been martyred. When she was about ten, Margaret and her family moved back to England, and she eventually married King Malcolm Gladmore (1058–93). To some, Margaret seems an anti-Celt. She replaced Gaelic with English in the royal court, and sought to eradicate any remaining differences between Christian practices in Scotland and the ones practised by her Benedictine chaplain, Turgot (who later wrote her hagiography). She worked to suppress 'barbarous practices' of the area, including a local liturgy of the Mass and avoidance of the sacraments (some monks so seriously held Paul's warning to the

'In essence, "Celtic Christianity" is a popular quest for a form of early British and Irish Christianity which is free from the great sins and failures of medieval and modern Christianity in the West.'

DONALD E. MEEK, 'SURVEYING THE SAINTS: REFLECTIONS ON RECENT WRITINGS ON "CELTIC CHRISTIANITY"', *SCOTTISH BULLETIN OF EVANGELICAL THEOLOGY*

Corinthian church against unworthily partaking of the eucharist that they had apparently stopped taking it altogether). One recent biographical sketch by a respected church historian said she 'succeeded in... ridding Scotland of Celtic church practices and bringing the country into the mainstream of Roman Catholicism'. At the same time, however, Margaret was fascinated by the religious history of her new country, especially monasticism. 'At that time very many men, shut up in cells apart, in various places of the Scots, were living in the flesh, but not according to the flesh; for they led the life of angels upon earth,' Turgot wrote. 'The queen endeavoured to venerate and love Christ in them; and to visit them very often with her presence and conversation and to commend herself to their prayers.' Margaret even rebuilt the monastery at Iona. Her reforms may not have been driven by cultural pride, but may have been an attempt to reclaim the spiritual rigour of Celtic Christianity's golden age.

Celtic Christianity also benefited during this period from a major development in Christianity around Europe: the rise of pilgrimage. Tales of monkish travel, especially the *Voyage of Brendan*, became popular around the Christian world. Meanwhile, pilgrimage points – some associated with historical events, others apparently made up during the time – reinforced stories of sanctity and spread them abroad. This was also the time when legends of King Arthur and the Holy Grail began circulating. As England and others in Christendom became enthralled with these tales, their imaginations were inflamed with thoughts of a magical Christian age before theirs.

The third revival period Bradley notes begins around 1250, as nationalist movements, especially those in Scotland, appropriated the saints. The apostle Andrew had grown into the symbol of Scottish independence, but Columba reportedly appeared to several kings, advising on military conquests. Relics of both Columba and the 8th-century monk Fillan were prominently used to rally Scottish troops at the battle of Bannockburn in 1314.

Scots at the Battle of Bannockburn invoked Columba and other saints in their efforts, reportedly parading around the Monymusk Reliquary (shown on page 157). Illustration from the *Holkham Picture Bible Book*.

National movements, however, were soon eclipsed by the Protestant Reformation, which shook the British Isles as it had the rest of Europe. At first, the Protestants rigorously opposed any association with the saints of old. Such devotion, they believed, smacked of idolatry. The first Protestant bishop of St David's in Wales, for example, even recommended that his headquarters be moved to another town to end the area's 'ungodly image service, abominable idolatry, and popish pilgrimage'. Relics were destroyed. Monasteries were closed. Someone even attacked Glastonbury's thorn tree, supposedly planted by Joseph of Arimathea himself. The Roman Catholics, meanwhile, begged Mary to 'awake Columba and Patrick' for help.

Protestants and Patrick

Starting with English reformer and Bible translator William Tyndale (c. 1494–1536), however, Protestants too saw their image reflected in the early Christian Celts. Christianity had found its way to the Celtic lands without any help from Rome, they argued. In fact, things only started to go wrong when Augustine showed up, in one reformer's words, 'to prepare Antichrist a seat here in England'. As archbishop of Canterbury Matthew Parker wrote in 1572:

There was a great difference between the Christianity of the Britons and the false Christianity which St Augustine of Canterbury gave the Saxons. The Britons kept their Christianity pure and immaculate, without admixture of human imaginings. Augustine's Christianity veered rather from the matchless purity of the Gospel and was mixed in with much superficiality, human opinions, and vain ceremonies, which did not accord with the nature of the kingdom of Christ.

James Ussher, the Calvinist archbishop of Armagh, is perhaps best known for his chronology of the Bible.

Few were more adamant in their belief that the Christian Celts were Protestants than Calvinist theologian James Ussher (1581–1656), appointed archbishop of Armagh in 1625. One of his first books, *A Discourse of the Religion anciently professed by the Irish*, sought to prove once and for all that 'the religion professed by the ancient bishops, priests, monks, and other Christians in this land, was for substance the very same' as his own.

Roman Catholics shot back with their own arguments about how they were the continuation of Celtic Christianity. These arguments continued through the centuries (and can still be heard today). But other forces – including patriotism, denominationalism and antiquarianism – joined in the 18th and 19th centuries to form what Ian Bradley sees as Celtic Christianity's fourth revivalist movement. It was also the time of Romanticists, who 'discovered' that Celtic Christianity fitted well with their ideology too. Romanticists were quick to assert that Celtic Christianity had much in common with pre-Christian Celtic beliefs. This belief actually began with the assertion that Celtic pagans 'had a religion so extremely like Christianity that in effect it differed from it only in this: they believed in a Messiah who was to come into this world, as we believe in him that is to come'. Modelled on Christian priests, the druids became described as the white-robed peacemongers so recognizable today.

De-Christianizing Celtic Christianity

By the end of the 1800s, Romanticists had switched the order – Christianity was a mere gloss on Celtic paganism. In a movement that W.B. Yeats called the 'Celtic Twilight', writers emphasized the Celts' love of nature over their love of Christ. Pantheism, not Christianity, was the true Celtic creed. Bradley notes that when George Russell wrote of Ireland 'long ago known as the sacred isle', he was not referring to the works of Patrick but to the fact that 'the gods lived there'.

Celticism had become more detached from Christianity in the Victorian era. 'Celtic Christianity was now chic [but] secularized and domesticated,' writes Bradley. 'Motifs that properly belonged on liturgical vessels were turning up on dressing tables and in drawing rooms... It is from this period that the fashion dates of wearing jewellery based on Celtic designs, and especially of pendants and necklaces in the form of Celtic crosses.'

The Celtic Twilight movement influenced the world's view of Celtic Christianity, but not everyone bought into its pantheistic views. What stuck were notions that the Celts had been ecologically minded, gentle, and at least friendly to the pagans they encountered. Many orthodox Christians,

'Ever since the early Christian monks of the Celtic Church set themselves the task of recording and adapting the achievements of Celtic paganism, a long line of Celtic antiquaries and scholars have devoted themselves to the same task right to the present day.'

NORMAN DAVIES,
THE ISLES

however, believed that this fitted well with their beliefs. One such person was Alexander Carmichael, the son of Scottish farmers from the island of Linsmore. A travelling taxman, Carmichael began befriending the locals he met on his journeys and wrote down thousands of prayers and blessings from their histories and memories. Published in six volumes between 1900 and 1961 (only the first two were edited and published during his lifetime), the *Carmina Gadelica* is still used today as a source for traditional Celtic Christian spirituality. Carmichael even found hymns sung before prayer:

*I am bending my knee
in the eye of the Father who created me,*

Celtic art themes made a comeback during the Victorian era.

in the eye of the Son who purchased me,
in the eye of the Spirit who cleansed me,
  in friendship and affection.
Through Thine own Anointed One, O God,
bestow upon us fullness in our need,
  love towards God,
  the affection of God,
  the smile of God,
  the wisdom of God,
  the grace of God,
  the fear of God,
  and the will of God
to do on the world of the Three,
as angels and saints
do in heaven;
  each shade and light,
  each day and night,
  each time in kindness,
  give Thou us Thy Spirit.

Another prayer echoes the *Lorica* falsely
attributed to Patrick. Carmichael heard it
from Mary Macrae, a 'brave kindly woman with her strong
Highland characteristics and her proud Highland spirit',
who danced and sang her traditional songs on the Isle of
Harris in the face of condemnation.

God with me lying down,
God with me rising up,
God with me in each ray of light,
nor I a ray of joy without Him,
  nor one ray without Him.

Christ with me sleeping,
Christ with me waking,
Christ with me watching,
every day and night,
  each day and night.

Alexander
Carmichael
(1832–1912).
'Religion, pagan
or Christian, or
both combined,
permeated
everything,' he
wrote in the
introduction
to his *Carmina
Gadelica*,
'blending and
shading into one
another like the
iridescent colours
of the rainbow.'

God with me protecting,
the Lord with me directing,
the Spirit with me strengthening,
for ever and for evermore.
  Ever and evermore, Amen.
    Chief of chiefs, Amen.

Carmichael's *Carmina Gadelica* has formed the backbone
of countless recent books on Celtic spirituality, but modern
academics complain that he apparently 'improved'
them after encountering them in the Highlands, making
fishermen and milkmaids speak with the euphonic, literary
style of late Victorian English. One scholar even accuses him
of trying to make the prayers sound as ancient as possible
when there was no reason for it. In any case, says Bradley:

The notion of a sacred deposit of religious poetry, originally
dating from the golden age of Celtic Christianity and still
surviving largely unchanged after nearly one a half millennia
of oral transmission from generation to generation, however
appealing, is difficult to sustain.

While Protestants continued to invoke the names of
Columba, Aidan and others in their opposition to Roman
Catholicism, a rising ecumenical movement also saw its
aims reflected as it gazed into the past. One of the leaders
of this movement was a Protestant minister from Glasgow
named George MacLeod. He convinced the governors of the
island of Iona to let him rebuild the Benedictine abbey on
the island, which had been closed since the Reformation. It
would be built in 1938 just as it had in Columba's time, by
volunteers and those who planned to live and work there
in community. It was not the only way that MacLeod
attempted to imitate the 6th-century Irish exile. 'The day,
organized with military precision, began with reveille at
6.45 a.m., and a swim [naked] in the freezing sea,' wrote
MacLeod's biographer. 'He insisted that the Celtic monks
bathed in the sea every day of the year and resisted the

arguments of faint-hearted ordinands who failed to see why they should slavishly follow masochistic Celtic customs.' Today more than 250,000 pilgrims visit the island annually, seeking what MacLeod called a 'thin place with only a tissue paper separating earth from heaven'.

The recent craze

Bradley dates the launch of the modern revival of Celtic Christianity to the early 1960s. Paperback anthologies began to take prayers of the *Carmina Gadelica* to the masses, writers began emphasizing Celtic theology and spirituality over interchurch rivalries, and marketers realized the potential of Celtic products, from albums

What happened to Whitby?

If the resurgence of Iona as a place of Celtic Christian revivalism illustrates the appropriation of the past, then Streanaeshalch (Whitby) may illustrate the neglect of it. For years, large pieces of the abbey graveyard have dropped onto the beach 150 feet below the old monastery. The cliffs Streanaeshalch sit on are too dangerous for archaeologists, so the graves of Hilda, Caedmon (the first Anglo-Saxon poet), and artefacts from King Oswy's era risked exposure, damage or irretrievable loss. Fortunately, a new, experimental digger was employed in 2001 to rescue the site. 'We've just got a tiny window of time to retrieve what could be vital clues about our past,' the English Heritage's Peter Busby told *The Guardian*. 'If we had left this dig any longer, an awful lot of history could have fallen into the North Sea and into oblivion.' Sadly, many associate the abbey not with history, but with Bram Stoker's fictional Dracula (who is shipwrecked near the abbey). The area visitors' centre is even emphasizing the vampire in its remodelling of its exhibits. The town of Whitby, meanwhile, has been a relatively prosperous fishing port since the Middle Ages.

of music to jewellery. By the 1980s, the Celtic craze was in full swing.

The Celtic Twilight movement's pro-pagan and syncretistic attitudes never set. Instead, many of today's books on the Celts – even ones focusing on Celtic spirituality after the cultural acceptance of Christianity – can be found in the neo-pagan, mythology, or New Age sections of bookstores. It is rarely because the books have been wrongly shelved. 'Far from rejecting their old religion, the Christian Celts continued to hold it in the deepest respect, absorbing many of its ideas and attitudes, symbols and rituals, into their new faith,' wrote Anglican priest Robert Van de Weyer in *Celtic Fire*. 'Christianity involved no change in moral belief.' (Patrick, who laments the attitudes of his pagan companions in his *Confessio*, may disagree.)

In her books *The Celtic Year* and *The Celtic Alternative*, Shirley Toulson sees the religion of the golden-age saints as reminiscent of many religions other than orthodox Christianity. After noting 'how much Celtic Christianity was open to the influence of 1st-century Judaism', Toulson asserts:

I am sure that if we want to understand the depths of Celtic spirituality we shall find the nearest parallels in the Buddhist teaching of today as well as in the creation spirituality of such Christian teachers as Matthew Fox [an excommunicated priest].

De-emphasizing the Christianity of Christian Celts has allowed these recent writers, like so many of their past revivalists, to emphasize their own agendas. The 'greenness' of the ancient saints is not a new concept, but it has taken a particular emphasis as environmentalism became more the vogue in the 1980s and 1990s. The point of view of writer John Matthews is clear from the title of one of his books *The Arthurian Tarot*. In another of his books, aimed at a more Christian subject, he writes:

When we read... the lives of the Celtic saints, we perceive the same fundamental truths that are present in the lives of the gods and heroes of the past: a love of the earth, of the pattern of the seasons, of the magical presence of animals, of the beauty of the revealed earth.

Theologically conservative Christians began reclaiming the Celtic saints as their own in the early 1990s. Leaders of the Church of England's charismatic movement were among the first to counter the neo-pagan and syncretistic approaches of their contemporaries and to encourage their evangelical comrades in drawing inspiration from the Celtic Christians. 'Evangelism, in Britain at least, has gained a bad name,' Ray Simpson laments in *Exploring Celtic Spirituality: Historic Roots for Our Future*. '[But] one thing that the Celtic churches had in common was a missionary spirit.' As a charismatic, Simpson also found similarities between Celtic Christianity and his movement's emphasis on spiritual warfare, miracles, healing, prophecy, and other spiritual gifts.

As interest in Celtic Christianity grew, Christians also began creating works 'in the Celtic tradition'. One of the key creators of this genre has been David Adam, vicar of Lindisfarne. His prayers echo the repetition of the *Carmina Gadelica, Loricae*, and other Celtic works: 'Blessed are you, Creator, and giver of peace. Peace be upon us; peace be upon this place; peace be upon this day. The deep, deep peace of God, which the world cannot give, be upon us and remain with us always.' Adam, however, is no Celt, and neither, notes Bradley, are most of the authors writing about Celtic Christianity in the current revival (including this author). Instead, they are:

... virtually all English, albeit in some cases with Celtic connections. It is reminiscent of the contribution made by Bede and the Anglo-Norman chroniclers... in the first two revivals. There is a similar agenda of romantic idealization, compounded by the certain guilt-induced acknowledgement

'It is indeed necessary for the church to address modern concerns, but the solutions lie not in a retreat to a mythical Celtic past, but, as always, in a sensitive Christian engagement with the present and the future.'

DONALD E. MEEK,
'MODERN MYTHS
OF THE
MEDIEVAL PAST',
CHRISTIAN HISTORY

of the validity of a marginalized tradition and a fascination with the 'outsider' and the 'other.'

This has provoked several modern historians to attack the modern fascination with Celtic Christianity as stuff and nonsense. 'From their southern perspectives, most of our writers reach out to embrace the northern "fringes" of the British Isles, often placing a great deal of emphasis on what might be termed the "purity of the periphery",' writes Donald Meek, chair of Celtic Studies at the University of Aberdeen. 'Those of us who inhabit the fringes find this kind of writing a little patronizing.'

Meek is one of the most vocal critics of the modern revival of Celtic Christianity, saying it has nothing to do with Christianity in the British Isles before 1100 and everything to do with wishful thinking:

'Celtic Christianity' in short, tends to scratch the many itches of our ecclesiastical bodies, public and personal. Given the profusion of our itches, it is hardly surprising that this interpretation of early Christianity in the British Isles crosses denominational, and even religious, boundaries.

Other scholars have gone even farther than Meek, suggesting that any concept of 'Celtic Christianity' past or present is a myth. Still, Meek and others do not see historical Celtic Christianity as untouchable, a practice best left on the shelf. 'There is much that all Christians can appreciate in the hymns, prayers, and stories of the Irish saints, although their message can be fully understood only be diligent scrutiny of the texts in their original forms,' he wrote. To this end, he and other historians are busy debunking myths and promoting areas of similarity, not difference, between Celtic Christians and their religious kindred on the continent.

These scholars are particularly frustrated with the modern revival's emphasis on Christian Celts as nature lovers. Many hagiographies are filled with stories of

'In the context of the current revival, it is tempting to suggest that Celtic Christianity is less an actual phenomenon defined in historical and geographical terms than an artificial construct created out of wishful thinking, romantic nostalgia, and the projection of all kinds of dreams about what should and might be.'

IAN BRADLEY,
*CELTIC CHRISTIANITY:
MAKING MYTHS AND
CHASING DREAMS*

A 12th-century
edition of
the *Life of
St Cuthbert*
shows the saint's
feet being dried
by otters as he
prays by the sea.

encounters with animals, but their purpose was rarely
to demonstrate the saints' environmental concerns.
Adomnán's tale of a crane visiting Iona is one of the most
cited evidences of the Celts' 'greenness'. At Columba's
order (for he had prophesied the crane's arrival), one of
the monks picked the crane up 'gently in its weakness, and
carried it to a dwelling that was near, where in its hunger he

fed it'. After three days of such care, the bird regained its strength and flew back to where it came from – Northern Ireland. But Adomnán was not demonstrating, as one writer argued, that 'hospitality means welcoming all God's creatures'. Instead, the hagiographer is attempting to show Columba's gift of prophecy. Meek points out another important reason for the story: 'Here Columba is affirming his Irish ancestral roots, and the crane acts as a specific link between the exile and his homeland.' Ignoring the meaning behind the tales is like taking Jesus' words, 'Consider the lilies of the field...' as an ecological command.

Modern environmentalists also ignore the past emphasis on dominion over creation. In the *Life of Columba*, the saint opposes nature more often than he indulges in it. 'Partly by mortification, and partly by a bold resistance, he subdued, with the help of Christ, the furious rage of wild beasts,' Adomnán writes in the third sentence of the hagiography. 'The surging waves, also, at times rolling mountains high in a great tempest, became quickly at his prayer quiet and smooth, and his ship, in which he then happened to be, reached the desired haven in a perfect calm.' Animals were used to illustrate God's (and the saints') power and holiness, but this was not unique to the Celts. Even Augustine of Hippo (whom Bradley says 'became the bogeyman for a new breed of pro-Celtic theologians who blamed him for giving Western Christianity its obsession with sin and guilt') revelled in natural splendours. 'With a great voice they cried out, "He made us",' he wrote. 'My question was the attention I gave to them; their response was their beauty.'

While acknowledging that 'wherever and whenever Christians are or have been found there have been differences in the ways they have believed and acted upon those beliefs,' historians are being careful to emphasize that these differences did not mean there was any thing like a 'Celtic church'. 'Far from being different, Celtic Christianity was very much like the faith of the church elsewhere,' says Dominican friar and scholar Gilbert Márkus:

There were differences in detail between the Celtic Christians and their continental neighbours: church architecture, Easter dates, inheritance laws, and local traditions. But almost all the main features of early Celtic Christianity could be found anywhere in Catholic Europe, where every tribe and tongue and nation made the gospel their own. The Celts found their own way of retelling the old story all the while sharing one recognizable faith.

That recognizable faith was not one that looked back at a golden age, even to the time of Jesus and the apostles. Instead, it was forward-looking, to the end of days. As Patrick wrote near the end of his *Confessio*:

For this sun which we now see rises each new day for us at [God's] command, yet it will never reign, nor will its splendour last forever. On the contrary, all who worship it today will be doomed to dreadful punishment. But we who believe and adore the true sun that is Christ, who will never die, nor will those who have done his will but abide forever just as Christ himself will abide for all eternity: who reigns with God the Father almighty, and with the Holy Spirit before time began, and now and through all ages of ages. Amen.

'Even if an authentic Celtic Christian culture is in a certain sense exclusive, and to a large degree a thing of the past, there are still all kinds of ways in which we may learn from this inheritance and make its wisdom our own.'

OLIVER DAVIES AND FIONA BOWIE, *CELTIC CHRISTIAN SPIRITUALITY*

Suggestions for Further Reading

As noted in Chapter 8, books on Celtic Christianity and 'spirituality' have been legion for more than a millennium, but the recent flood of titles since the mid-1990s is enough to overwhelm even the fondest enthusiast. One of the best overviews – for both readability and academic credibility – dates from just before this most recent fascination. Some of the information in J.T. McNeill's *The Celtic Churches* (University of Chicago, 1974) is now outdated, but I am heavily indebted to his narrative work for this volume.

As ancient documents go, the primary source material for the ancient Celtic saints holds up remarkably well for the modern reader. There are, of course, several excellent translations of Patrick's *Confessio* and *Letter to the Soldiers* of Coroticus (such as John Skinner's, Doubleday, 1998), and some new publications – Máire B. de Paor's *Patrick* (Veritas, 1998) and Thomas O'Loughlin's *Saint Patrick* (Triangle, 1999) include fascinating notes.

Celtic Spirituality (Paulist Press, 1999) includes Patrick's works of course, but it is invaluable for its other primary source materials; Oliver Davies's translations of hagiographies, penitentials, poetry, sermons and other works is invaluable. Liam de Paor's *Saint Patrick's World* (Four Courts Press, 1993) and Uinseann Ó Maindín's *The Celtic Monk* (Cistercian Press, 1996) also let the Celtic Christians speak for themselves.

Most books on Celtic Christianity concentrate on the lives of a few extraordinary saints and use the daily life of monastic communities only to illustrate the sanctity of their subjects. Lisa Bitel's *Isle of the Saints* (Cornell University Press, 1990) instead focuses on 'ordinary' life at these monasteries, from the role of food to views of labour. Meanwhile, Richard J.

Woods's *The Spirituality of the Celtic Saints* (Orbis, 2000) attempts to draw attention to lesser-known leaders of the faith.

A host of books combine rich illustrations with reliable history to tell the story of the pre-Christian Celts. Among the better ones are Simon James's *The World of the Celts* (Thames and Hudson, 1993) and Barry Cunliffe's *The Celtic World* (St Martin's Press, 1990).

Other helpful books include:

Bede, translated by Leo Sherley-Price, *A History of the English Church and People*, Penguin, 1955.

Ian Bradley, *Celtic Christianity: Making Myths and Chasing Dreams*, St Martin's Press, 1999.

John B. Bury, *The Life of St Patrick and His Place in History*, Macmillan, 1905.

Thomas Cahill, *How the Irish Saved Civilization*, Doubleday, 1995.

T.M. Charles-Edwards, *Early Christian Ireland*, Cambridge University Press, 2000.

Norman Davies, *The Isles: A History*, Oxford University Press, 1999.

Oliver Davies and Fiona Bowie, *Celtic Christian Spirituality: An Anthology of Medieval and Modern Sources*, Continuum, 1995.

Denise Dersin (ed.), *What Life Was Like Among Druids and High Kings*, Time Life, 1998.

James P. Mackey (ed.), *An Introduction to Celtic Christianity*, T&T Clark, 1995.

Thomas O'Loughlin, *Journeys on the Edges: The Celtic Tradition*, Darton, Longman and Todd, 2000.

Thomas O'Loughlin, *Celtic Theology: Humanity, World and God in Early Irish Writings*, Continuum, 2000.

Máire de Paor and Liam de Paor, *Early Christian Ireland*, Thames and Hudson, 1958.

Steve Rabey, *In the House of Memory: Ancient Celtic Wisdom for Everyday Life*, Dutton Press, 1998.

Katherine Scherman, *The Flowering of Ireland: Saints, Scholars and Kings*, Little, Brown and Co., 1981.

Edward C. Sellner, *Wisdom of the Celtic Saints*, Ave Maria Press, 1993.

Index

A

Adam, David 179–80
Adomnán 103, 106, 109–14, 117–20, 155, 168, 181–82
Aelred 45–46
Aidan of Iona 117
Aidan of Lindisfarne 113–15, 150, 154, 169, 176
Alban 37–42, 81
Alexander the Great 16
Ammianus Marcellinus 15
Antony of Egypt 44, 48, 52
Ardagh Chalice 4
Aristotle 16
Arthur, King 36, 48–49, 170
Athanasius 44
Augustine of Canterbury 145–45, 172
Augustine of Hippo 43, 56, 81, 182

B

Bede 40, 42, 45, 56, 108, 112, 113, 117, 119, 138–39, 145, 147–56, 168–69
Bitel, Lisa 81, 132
Blake, William 35
Blandina 31–32
Blathmac 156
Boniface 142
Boniface IV, Pope 133–34
Book of Kells 106, 156–59, 168
Bradley, Ian 168–80
Brendan of Clonfert 121–26, 138, 170
Brennus 7, 11–12
Brigid 94, 95–99, 106, 124
Brunhilde 134

C

Cahill, Thomas 6, 105, 167–68
Candida Casa (the white house), Whithorn 45–47, 79, 105, 115
Cannera 99
Carmichael, Alexander 174–77
Celestine, Pope 56–57

Céli Dé (Clients of God) 87, 94, 95
Celtic languages 18
Celtic Twilight 173, 178–79
Clancy, Thomas 45
Claudius, Emperor 37
Colmán of Lindisfarne 150–54
Columba 7, 103–15, 117, 118, 124, 151, 154, 156–57, 170, 182
  death of 114–15
  founds Iona 106–109
Columbanus 34, 130–38, 147–48
Comgall of Bangor 87, 94–95, 106, 124, 132
Constantius Chlorus 40
Council of Arles 42–44, 145
Council of Basle 35
Council of Nicea 146
Croagh Patrick 76
Cummian 148
Cuthbert 118
Cyprian of Carthage 34

D

David of Wales (Dewi) 7, 51–54
Decius, Emperor 40
Delphi 16
Diocletian, Emperor 40, 43
Diodorus Siculus 10, 13, 15, 26, 27
druids 24, 26, 28–29, 61, 71–72, 97, 98, 112, 114, 149, 173
Dubricus (Dyfrig) 49

E

Easter 43, 71, 109, 123, 132, 145–47
Egbert 155–56
Eigg 161
Énda 79, 124
environmentalism 180–82
Eusebius 36

F

Fiacra 141–42
Fillan 170
Finnian of Clonard 105
Finnian of Moville 103, 105
food 13
Fursa 138–41

G

Gaius Marius 16
Galatia, Galatians 29–30
Gall 135–38
Germanus of Auxerre 56, 59, 66
Gildas the Wise 7, 36, 54–55, 124
Gregory I, Pope (Gregory the Great) 133, 143
Gregory II, Pope 142
Gregory of Tours 34
Gundestrup cauldron 27

H

Hadrian's Wall 37–39
Hallstatt 20–21
Hilda of Whitby 150, 154, 177
Hill of Tara 71–72, 104
Holy Grail 36, 170

I

Iceland 126–29
Illtud 49–51, 54, 129
Innocent I, Pope 56
Iona 108–109, 113–18, 124, 154–57, 164, 170, 176–77, 181
Irenaeus 32–33
Íte 98, 124

J

Jerome 29–30, 56
Jesus 30, 35, 44, 67, 68, 84, 95, 132, 146, 154, 182, 183
John Paul II, Pope 77
Joseph of Arimathea 35–36
Julius Caesar 16–18, 22–24, 26, 28, 29, 37

K

Kevin of Glendalough 82–85, 99

L

La Tène 19–20
Laurence of Canterbury 147, 148
Law of the Innocents 118–20, 155, 185
Leo, Pope 133
Lindisfarne 116–17, 157, 169, 179
Lindow Man 25–26
Livy 11, 12

Loch Ness monster 112
Loiguire 71–73
Lorica ('Patrick's Breastplate') 73, 99
Lucretius 11
Lyons 31–33

M

MacLeod, George 176–77
Marcus Aurelius 31, 33
Margaret, Queen of Scotland 169–70
Martial 30
Martin of Tours 44–45
martyrdom 31–33, 40–42, 80–81, 109
Meek, Donald 179, 180–82
Monenna 99
Monymusk Reliquary 157
Muiredach Cross 1

N

Nennius 48
Ninian (Uinniau) 45–47
Non 51
Norman conquest 169

O

O'Loughlin, Thomas 78, 146
Olaf the Red (Anlaf Curran) 164
Olaf Trygvesson 161
Origen of Alexandria 36
Orwell, George 12
Oswy, King of Northumbria 148–55

P

paganism 26–29, 173, 178
Palladius 56–60
Parker, Matthew 172
Patrick 7, 58–79, 80, 97, 99, 101, 118, 124, 160, 173, 183
    and eschatology 67–70
    and monasteries 76–77
    and paganism 70
    and slavery 74–75
    death of 77–78
    escapes from slavery 61–65
    return to Ireland 65–67
    taken into slavery 60–61

Paul   29–30, 67, 70, 169
Pelagius   55–57, 81
Peloponnesian War   16
penitentials   87–89
Pliny   19
Polybius   18
Pomponius Mela   29
Poseidonius   13
Pothinus   31–32
prayer   89–91
Protestant Reformation   171–73

Q

Quartodecimans   146

R

rivalries   99–102
Rome
    sack of   11–12
    withdrawal from Britain   47, 60
Ronán   129–30
rules, monastic   53, 87–89, 90–91, 94

S

Samson of Dol   50–51, 129
scholarship   91–93
Septimus Severus   40
Siegfried, King   118
Sigebert I, King   138
Simpson, Ray   179
Skellig Michael   2, 85, 87
soul friend (*anamchara*)   93–95
Strabo   13, 19, 23, 28, 29
Sylvester, Pope   145
Symphorian of Autun   33
Synod of Hertford   155
Synod of Whitby   148–56

T

Táin Bó Cuailgne   7
Tara brooch   9
Tertullian   36
Tiberius Caesar   36–37
Tolkien, J.R.R.   6
tonsure   149
Turgesius   163–64
Tyndale, William   172

U

Ussher, James   172

V

Vercingetorix   23
Vettius Epagathus   31
Vikings   7, 156–64

W

West Virginia   127
Wilfrid   151–55
William of Malmesbury   36
Woods, Richard   48

Y

Yeats, W.B.   173

Picture and Text Acknowledgments

Pictures

Picture research by Zooid Pictures Limited.

AKG – London: pp. 12 (Peter Connolly), 13 (Erich Lessing), 27 (Erich Lessing), 49 (British Library), 68–69, 93 (British Library), 107 (Trinity College, Dublin), 116 (British Library), 122 (British Library), 144 (British Library), 158 (Trinity College, Dublin).

The Board of Trinity College Dublin: pp. 40–41.

Bridgeman Art Library: pp. 4 (National Museum of Ireland, Dublin, Ireland), 14, 17 (British Museum), 118 (British Library), 181 (British Library).

Corbis UK Ltd: pp. 1 (Andrea Jemolo), 2–3 (Michael St Maur Sheil), 22 (Bettmann), 28 (Hulton-Deutsch Collection), 32–33 (Todd Gipstein), 38–39 (Adam Woolfitt), 62–63 (Michael Neveux), 77 (Tim Thompson), 79, 82–83 (Richard Cummins), 86 (Farrell Grehan), 110–11 (Wild Country), 117 (Michael Nicholson), 128 (Charles & Josette Lenars), 162 (Sean Sexton Collection), 172 (Bettmann).

Fortean Picture Library: p. 120 (Andreas Trottmann).

Hulton Archive/Getty Images: p. 56.

Heritage Image Partnership: pp. 25 (The British Museum), 66 (The British Library), 149 (The British Library).

LLT Productions: p. 137.

Mick Sharp Photography: pp. 45, 46, 52–53, 54–55, 152–53.

National Museums of Scotland: pp. 157, 175.

National Museum of Ireland: pp. 8, 70.

Newry & Mourne District Council: p. 99 (courtesy of Newry & Mourne District Council).

Photo Resource UK: p. 21 (C.M. Dixon).

Robert L. Pyle: pp. 126–27.

The Royal Irish Academy: p. 103 (by permission of the Royal Irish Academy, copyright © RIA).

Stiftsbibliothek St Gallen: p. 135.

Victoria & Albert Museum: p. 174.

Werner Forman Archive: pp. 10–11 (British Museum), 104–105, 125, 161 (Viking Ship Museum, Bygdoy).

Derek West: maps on pp. 20–21, 100, 140–41.

Text

Extracts from Bede are translated by Leo Sherley-Price and are taken from *A History of the English Church and People*, Penguin, 1955.

Extracts from Patrick's works are taken from the following sources:

St Patrick: The Man and His Works by Thomas O'Loughlin, SPCK, 1999.

The Confession of St Patrick, translated by John Skinner, Image/Doubleday, 1998.

Celtic Spirituality by Oliver Davies, Paulist Press, 1999.

Saint Patrick's World by Liam De Paor, Four Courts Press, 1993.

Other extracts:

p. 73: The *Lorica*, translated by Oliver Davies. Text in *Thesaurus Palaeohibernicus*, edited by Whitely Stokes and John Strachan, Cambridge, 1903, 2:296. Taken from *Celtic Christian Spirituality: An Anthology of Medieval and Modern Sources*, edited by Oliver Davies and Fiona Bowie, Continuum, 1995, copyright © 1995 Oliver Davies and Fiona Bowie. Reprinted by permission of the Continuum International Publishing Group and SPCK.

pp. 81–82: 'All alone in my little cell…' translated by Oliver Davies, from *Kuno*

Meyer, Eriu 2, pp. 55–56. Taken from *Celtic Christian Spirituality: An Anthology of Medieval and Modern Sources*, edited by Oliver Davies and Fiona Bowie, Continuum, 1995, copyright © 1995 Oliver Davies and Fiona Bowie. Reprinted by permission of the Continuum International Publishing Group and SPCK.

p. 89: 'Psalm-singer, beginning student...' translated from *Kuno Meyer, 'Mitteilungen au irischen Handschriften'*, ZCP 5, 1905, pp. 498–99. Taken from *Isle of the Saints*, copyright © 1990 Lisa Bitel. Used by permission of the publisher, Cornell University Press.

p. 90: 'Lord, be it thine...' translated by Robin Flower, from *Poems and Translations*, The Lilliput Press, Dublin, 1995.

p. 91: 'The clear-voiced bell...' translated by Robin Flower, from *Poems and Translations*, The Lilliput Press, Dublin, 1995.

p. 91: 'A hedge of trees...' translated by Gerard Murphy. Taken from *Early Irish Lyrics*, Oxford University Press, 1956 and Four Courts Press, 1998. Reproduced by kind permission of the estate of Gerard Murphy and Four Courts Press.

pp. 91–92: 'I and Pangur Bán...' from 'The Student and His White Cat', translated by Robin Flower, from *Poems and Translations*, The Lilliput Press, Dublin, 1995.

pp. 174–76: 'I am bending my knee...' and 'God with me lying down...' from *Carmina Gadelica, Hymns and Incantations from the Gaelic*, collected and edited by Alexander Carmichael, Floris Books, Edinburgh 1992, and Lindisfarne Books, Hudson, NY, 1992.